U.S.A.
THE
PERMANENT
REVOLUTION

U.S.A.

THE
PERMANENT
REVOLUTION

*By the Editors of Fortune
in collaboration with
Russell W. Davenport*

New York
PRENTICE-HALL
1951

E
169
.1
.F75

CONTENTS

INTRODUCTION

IT IS A TRUISM of current speculation on world affairs that the role of the U.S.A. is crucial. On this point, indeed, the world would seem to have achieved unanimity; nowhere does anyone argue that American policy does not matter. But as with other truisms, we begin to run into difficulties as soon as we examine this one. In just what respect is American policy important? Or, to put the question more concretely, what is America supposed to do about her importance? What ends should she serve, what goals should she pursue?

Here the American isolationists, who are often no more than would-be nationalists, think they have an answer. America, they contend, should serve her own ends exclusively. She should pursue her own goals. But what are the American goals? Around that question all policy must revolve. There is much evidence to show that if Americans knew their goals they could very likely attain them. They have vast power—moral, military, and economic—and they have a tradition of success. But the unhappy fact is that just at this juncture in world affairs the American goals are not clear. Almost nothing in the way of a goal has emerged from current thinking beyond the

vii

purely negative *objective* (which is something less than a goal) of "containing" the U.S.S.R. and "stopping" red Communism.

Rarely have a people with so great a tradition been reduced in a time of crisis to so sterile an aim. And when one inquires as to how this tragic circumstance has come about, one finds still another question lurking behind the question of goals. This question has to do with the *meaning* of the U.S.A. What, as a nation, are we all about? Perhaps we know, but if so, the confusion of ideas regarding America is somewhat startling. The truth seems to be that Americans of this generation have in a profound sense lost touch with their own meaning; and this is nowhere better illustrated than in the fact that they appear to be incapable of explaining it to anybody else. Neither the cultural nor the political leadership of America has been able to clarify the meaning of America with authority. In fact, the nearest approaches to clarification have come, ironically enough, from military leaders and business leaders—two groups that are not supposed to possess much "enlightenment" in such matters. General Eisenhower, for example, has managed to convey to the people of Europe (and to Americans themselves) more concrete ideas of the meaning of America than has the State Department. And Paul G. Hoffman, formerly head of ECA and now director of the Ford Foundation, is an example of a businessman who has managed to express something like an American meaning to most of the nations of the earth.

The general bankruptcy concerning this question is revealed at every meeting of men and women, convened, whether formally or informally, to discuss any aspect of American policy or to plan out anything for the future. Such a discussion always runs up against the question of goals, and, if this question is pursued, the question of what America really *is*. Someone always calls upon somebody else to produce the answer to this. Books and articles are written demanding a "philosophy." Other books ask for a "spiritual revival." Organizations like Freedoms Foundation seek to "revive" the spirit of Valley Forge. And so forth. Everyone is demanding to hear the truth. But who is shedding the light of truth?

Or does anybody believe in truth? That really has become a question. The relativistic nature of modern thinking, which has dominated intellectuals and woven itself into our entire educational system, has resulted in a kind of fragmentation of belief, so that no one dares to speak except in terms of individual opinion. All general concepts are thus undermined; they are dismissed as "transcendental" and thereby denied "reality." The result is a social fabric created almost entirely of woof, with little warp in it; a banner that quickly frays to mere threads when lifted in the wind.

The question itself of the *meaning* of America is, indeed, a prime case in point. Why should we assume that America has *any* meaning? Is not the U.S.A. a nation? And does a nation have any meaning other than the fact that it is a nation? What "meaning" does Britain have, for example, other than that she is Britain; or France, other than that she is France? A nation is an aggregate of people who have banded together under certain governmental forms, to assure their survival and promote their interests. What other meaning can America have?

This kind of pragmatic thinking casts a powerful spell over the modern mind. Yet by any criterion of truth, whether scientific or intuitional, it falls far short. Leaving aside the questions of Britain and France, which are not within our province here, it is overwhelmingly evident that America *always has had* a meaning for Americans (and indeed, for most of the world) over and above the merely national. This fact can be documented to any desired extent in the utterances of American leaders, from the very beginning until now; and some of the documentation is presented in the following pages. Yet one need not rely merely on the leaders. A little careful observation of the puzzled discussion groups already mentioned, which gather around the dinner table or the conference table, reveals the *assumption* in virtually everyone's mind that a trans-national meaning exists. The pure nationalist is a rarity in America. On the contrary, the very puzzlement of such groups arises from the inner knowledge that American policy cannot be merely national, but must, to be valid, relate itself to humanity as a whole. This relationship, were it known, would embody the meaning of America. By means of it—if we knew it—our goals could be defined. And by reference to those goals we could then make policy.

For something more than twenty years the editors of FORTUNE have observed the intellectual and spiritual confusion that has led to the present bankruptcy of U.S. policy that so enervates the world. They have indeed been part of it. They have lived it. They accept their share of the responsibility for it. Yet in their studies of America, chiefly in the field of business and industry, and also somewhat in the related field of politics, they have become increasingly aware of the existence, in the very midst of modern America, of certain general principles, the reality of which—however metaphysical—is extremely difficult to deny. These principles, of course, are not in the least new. Their roots go back two thousand years or so. Western history is largely the story of their development, in which every western—and many eastern—nations were involved. Then, in the eighteenth century, by an extraordinary concatenation of circumstance and talent, they were brilliantly formulated, in the language of that day, by the men responsible for founding the U.S.A. The language in which they were couched may seem to modern ears somewhat quaint. But this does not mean that the principles are quaint. It is the language, the way of thinking, that has changed, not the principles. These, we find, remain dynamically at work in our society. They have been transformed, but they are not dead; on the contrary, they embody the meaning of America just as much as they ever did. And if we want to discover that meaning, so that we can define our goals, so that we can formulate our policies, our first task is to turn to them with an open-minded and open-hearted attitude; to try to make them clear for ourselves and the rest of the world.

In the light of these reflections the authors present the present work with no little humility, conscious that it represents the merest beginning—perhaps, indeed, no more than an introduction to the general approach suggested above. *U.S.A.: The Permanent Revolution* was originally published as the February, 1951, issue of FORTUNE magazine. The generous reception of that issue is what encouraged us to present it as a book. But we are keenly aware that in its present form it exhibits the defects of its journalistic origin. Since it was written as a magazine, the reader will find a certain lack of continuity between the chapters, each of which was originally composed as an article in its own right. He will find, also, a kind of condensation that is more proper to journalism than to literature. And he will perhaps feel the lack of any grand summing-up of the major theme.

If, however, this book serves even as an adequate introduction to a general reconsideration, in modern terms, of certain truths about America, we shall consider ourselves justified in publishing it. Indeed, we might well call it a series of introductions to various aspects of the meaning of the U.S.A., as if a searchlight were hurriedly to probe different sectors of a dark terrain. The illumination of the whole we must leave to the people and their political philosophers, hoping that our searchlight will have revealed at least enough to stimulate them to undertake that formidable task.

Another defect may be found in the fact that our theme presents the U.S.A. in terms so glowing as to be offensive to foreign ears. Here, too, we plead the limitations of the medium for which the work was originally written. In each of the original articles we were not so much concerned with the feelings of our foreign friends as with certain realities that Americans themselves have tended to overlook; and our effort in every case was to portray these in their positive aspects. Beyond this, however, it seems to us incontestable that the importance of America to the rest of the world has to do not merely with American economic and military power, but with the fact that Americans may yet be able to solve some of the social, economic, and political problems that have been tearing the free world apart. No responsible American should presume to tell other people how they must solve their problems—and such is not in the least our intention here. But it is certainly no disservice to set forth for other people some of the major factors that may enable us to solve some of our own.

This point, we feel, deserves little argument. On one point only, indeed, will we take serious issue with those who criticize this book for being too aggressively "American." This has to do with what we have called the "universals" that underlie the American system. The objection will doubtless be raised that Americans have no right to claim universality for anything in their system. But this objection we would resist. We do not present the universals in question as Americans. They pertain, we contend, to no nation, but to humanity. Just as much as the principles of science, for example, they are common to all men. And therefore the question of Americans thrusting them upon anybody can never really arise. Either we are wrong in our judgment that they are universals, in which case they will fall; or else we are right, in which case humanity will awaken to them of its own accord. Meanwhile, the concept of America as a guardian of these universals remains, in our judgment, historically incontestable. Though Americans hate war, they have now entered two world conflicts, the ultimate purpose of which was the exercise of that guardianship.

There is much evidence to show, we believe, that the world is even now awakening to those very universals that America has always undertaken to guard. What is called the "unrest" of Asia is a symptom of this awakening—though Asiatics would phrase the universals in question quite differently. So it is throughout most of the non-Communist world. In different civilizations different aspects of the awakening are manifest, different problems encountered: but the awakening has to do, we believe, with what we have called the permanent revolution. What, indeed, is western Europe struggling for, if it is not for the realization, in European terms, of the very universals which constitute the foundation of freedom here? The great revolution out of which the U.S. was born, and to the furtherance of which all of its vital institutions are in fact dedicated—the revolution of the human individual against the tyrannies of nature and of man, of force and darkness—was first begun in Europe, and in a certain sense belongs to Europe even more than it does to America. The special opportunities opened up on this continent, both political and economic, imposed upon Americans the role of guarding the revolutionary principles. But Americans alone cannot *realize* them. Their realization is a joint task for the peoples of the earth, in the performance of which Europe must play a critical role.

It would be a just criticism, we think, that this book leaves the nature of these universals somewhat obscure.

It does not elaborate on them. Only the first three chapters deal with them in a direct way; the bulk of the book is concerned primarily with American applications. In a certain sense we should *like* this criticism to be made, because it might indicate a desire on the part of competent persons to inquire further into the principles in question. For we are convinced that in them the meaning of America is to be found.

In fact, we offer the following somewhat startling hypothesis: that the changes in American society, which appear to have been so radical since the days of the founders, have been brought about, not by disregard for the founders' principles, but by the instinctive application of them. *Rightly understood, the principles that embody the meaning of America are the very forces that have done most to change America.* Those who have been living in the delusion that these principles are "outgrown" had better think that one over.

If this hypothesis is correct, it leads us out to a helpful conclusion. It enables us to see that American policy cannot be solved in purely defensive terms. Such a course as that recently proposed by Herbert Hoover, for example, which speaks of the U.S. as a kind of "Gibraltar," is very wide of the mark. American freedom cannot be defended in that way. American freedom has its being in principles which do not belong to America but to the world. Our whole evolution is based on the action of these principles, and our hope of future solutions rests upon our further ability to apply them. To withdraw is to undermine ourselves. And to define our "defense" in purely military terms is to deny ourselves the further development of *our own* free institutions.

In the last analysis, then, if the hypothesis in question is accepted, the formulation of a sound policy for America involves spiritual as well as military and economic considerations: not in the sense of denominational religion, however important that may be, but in the sense that we must continually rediscover within ourselves, and continually learn to implement, those universal human principles of which our version of freedom has been created. Without these principles we cannot hope to be free. Yet we cannot hope to understand them if we consider them exclusively our own. The isolationist cliché that America should serve her own ends exclusively has little meaning when viewed in this light. We must so frame our policies that we may discover in ourselves, as individuals, and learn to implement, that which we hold in common with all humanity.

There come times in the history of every people when destiny knocks on their door with an iron insistence. In the history of America, destiny has knocked thus three times: once when we faced the seemingly impossible odds of British power to gain our independence: once at Fort Sumter, when we faced the bloody task of preserving our union: and it is knocking today.

It is true that on other grave occasions Americans have heard the knock of destiny. They heard it in 1917 when they sent their first expeditionary force to Europe. They heard it even more loudly in 1941, when they were roused out of an isolationist lethargy to fight—again against odds—one of the most brilliant and important wars in history. Yet on neither of those occasions did the knocking have the iron clang that we hear today. In World War I, and even in World War II, a mold existed into which we could pour our vast energies. Our power— and in the second war our leadership also—was essential to victory. But it was not our task to make the mold. It was not our task to determine either the geographical contours or the moral content of the battle. That had already been done by the rest of the world.

But today, though we again have allies, though we have the United Nations, though we have access to resources all over the world, it is *we* who must shape the struggle: *we* must make the mold. That is the meaning of the iron clang. Our outlook is the same as it was at the time of the Revolution, and again at the time of the Civil War: the shape of things to come depends on us: our moral decision, our wisdom, our vision, and our will.

R. W. D.

PART I.

The U.S. is not merely a nation but a Way of Life founded on a universal Proposition. In this part the Proposition is stated and the resulting System defined.

THE AMERICAN
WAY OF LIFE

WHEN A FRENCHMAN wants to explain his country he speaks simply of *"la belle France."* The Britisher says, "There'll always be an England." These and other nations of the earth can tell a lot about themselves just by the use of their proper names. But the citizen of the U.S. has a different problem. There lives in him a kind of unspoken assumption that his nation is something more than a nation; that it is an experiment, perpetually evolving into something new; that it embodies an ideal. In referring to his country, therefore, he feels the need of including an abstraction or a general principle; and this leads him on a quest for words.

The best he has ever found is "Liberty"; but for reasons explained in "Individualism Comes of Age" (Chapter XI), the rise of the social problem has somewhat tarnished the sheen of this greatest of all American abstractions. In the last century there was something called "Manifest Destiny." From time to time someone always comes up with "the American Dream." But these phrases do violence to another favorite Americanism, common sense. As a result, when Americans of the mid-twentieth century want to refer in an inclusive way to all that vast complex of manners, customs, techniques, ideas, laws, and principles that they know as the U.S., they take refuge in a vague but tantalizing abstraction that they call "the American Way of Life."

Precise thinkers detest this phrase. It is used by every orator on every side of every issue; by the labor leader haranguing his local, the businessman squeezed into an elevator on his way up to a metropolitan luncheon club, the dentist flourishing his drill at a patient who is trying not to think. It is used beyond our shores by pundits and intellectuals—and there, indeed, lies the rub. For "the American Way of Life," besides being a vague phrase, is an ambiguous one. It seems to imply that those who advocate it wish to impose on the rest of the world all that which goes to make up a "way of life," all the customs and manners, the economic practices and the governmental forms—all the *particulars*—that make America what it is. But this is as far from the truth as anything could be. Americans never have advocated, and so long as they faithfully practice their "way of life" never will advocate, the imposition on other peoples of the American particulars.

The phrase gets the American into other difficulties, too. In a way, it sets him apart from the rest of the human race, as if he had taken up residence on another planet.

4

This aspect of the matter worries him deeply. In the first place, he likes to be liked—indeed, he carries his craving for popularity and human "acceptance" to extremes that are sometimes pathetic. Besides, he really likes people. Then there is this ideal of his, which is a human ideal, not a national or a racial ideal. All these factors combine to make the American feel that he is very much a part of *this* planet. He is proud that his country is populated by so many races and national origins. He welcomes into his midst their various cultures and traditions. He cherishes a liking for many distant peoples—the Chinese, for instance, have always been favorites of his (and the fact that he is fighting them now is a tragic incongruity). Finally, he is taking very seriously his new role of leadership in the Western world, whose culture and spiritual traditions form the basis of his own, and whose civilization he is prepared to defend. The idea that he, of all people, wants to be set apart from the rest of humanity is a mockery of the way he really feels.

Thus this phrase, "the American way of life," however useful for certain purposes, has become productive of a great deal of misunderstanding and friction. But on the other hand, it would not be practical to abandon it, because it does mean something important—indeed, to the American, something indispensable. So the only way to proceed is to try to clear up the misunderstanding. And this in turn involves an understanding of what the American way of life is really like. It involves an understanding, specifically, of the all-important fact that this phase is comprised of two important elements: one, the particulars which Americans do not expect other peoples to

5

share with them, inasmuch as they are peculiar to Americans; the other, certain universals which Americans believe belong to all mankind and the nature of which it is the American task to unfold.

To the foreign visitor the most disturbing thing about the American way of life is its unabashed "materialism." The visitor is drenched with sights and sounds and smells emanating from a man-made environment to which almost all Americans appear to give almost all their energies. Pervading these sensory experiences there are the psychological ones—the insouciant way in which the radio combines "entertainment" with the most humiliating requirements of the human organism—the ubiquitous advertising, seeking to identify human happiness with bright teeth—the infantile movie heroes—the wasteful "abundance" protruding from every retail store. The visitor sees all this, and is impelled to somber speculations concerning the fate of humanity. What price "the American Way of Life"?

The somber speculations lead to two forms of criticism. The first, fanned by Mr. Vishinsky, runs to the effect that American capital exists for the purpose of exploiting the people, who have thereby been degraded. This attack, however, is an easy one to meet. It may be a halfway adequate picture of what capitalism in America used to be like, or of what it is still like in some places today. But it no more fits modern America than a description of the living habits of Caesar.

The U.S. Bureau of Labor Statistics maintains a Consumers' Price Index, which is intended to show changes

in the current cost of living, and which is therefore composed of the index levels of all articles that enter into
the cost of living in an important way. This index, which
is compiled specifically for "moderate income families,"
has for years included radios, electric sewing machines,
electric refrigerators, vacuum cleaners, automobiles,
tires, gasoline, and insurance; medical, dental, surgical,
and hospital care; drugs and beauty-shop services—all
this, that is to say, over and above necessities like food,
clothing, and shelter. But the BLS has felt for some time
that this index was deficient; certain items, important
enough materially to affect the cost of living, were not
included. These, therefore, have been added. They include television sets, electric toasters, frozen foods,
canned baby foods, home permanent-wave lotions, and
group hospitalization contracts. As the New York *Herald
Tribune* wryly remarked, "What, no caviar?"

Now to talk of the exploitation of human needs, in an
economy where all these items have become so important to the standard of living that they must be figured
into the cost of living, is to talk nonsense. The American capitalistic system still works injustices; but to think
of it in terms of exploitation is to think in terms of a past
century. It is perfectly evident from the above list that
it is not the capitalists who are using the people, but the
people who are using the capitalists. Capital has become,
not the master of this society, but its servant. No better
evidence could be adduced than the figures recently
made public by the Federal Reserve Board, which show
that four out of ten American families possess at least
$5,000 of assets over liabilities; and that very nearly one

7

family in ten has net assets of $25,000 or more. It is not just a capitalistic system. It is a capitalistic people.

But this raises the second form of criticism. If the trouble isn't with the capitalists, then it must be with the people. Men and women who insist on such a high standard of living, and are willing to expend so much energy to get it, must be hopeless materialists. Is it not true that the curse of this majestic continent is the drab uniformity of its products and the discouraging *con*formity of its mores? The itinerant lecturer is especially exposed to this dreary prospect. On his way from town to town he sees the same ads for the same products; he hears the same clichés; he is asked the same question by people who look and act and dress and entertain themselves, apparently, in exactly the same way as the people in the town he thought he had left behind him—the name of whose central thoroughfare, incidentally, was also Main Street. If this is "freedom," thinks the itinerant lecturer, then what is all the shouting and ballyhoo about? There are quicker ways to build an anthill.

Now the American admits that his society is materialistic; that standardization is an essential of the "way of life"; that conformity is a danger he must watch and learn to counteract. Nevertheless, this criticism from the itinerant lecturer baffles him on the whole, because it seems to overlook more than it takes into account. For example, it overlooks the great American love of *diversity*.

The American responds to diversity as to something good, absolutely. The presence in his society of a bewildering number of races and national origins, creeds

8

and shibboleths, economic interests and explosive ideas, is to him no problem at all. On the contrary, it is a great asset. In his labyrinthine political system the same idea is carried out. The forty-eight states, each with its separate constitution and different set of laws, each requiring special examinations or licenses for its lawyers, its doctors, its civil servants, even its automobile drivers, confront the foreigner as an irrationally complicated structure calculated to produce nothing but chaos. But the American thinks it is good, he can even prove that it is good. If there is only one of something, he is suspicious of it—as for example his federal government. This is only partly because he dreads the power of monopoly, whether political or economic. It is also because he sees diversity as the expression of freedom, the living proof that men and women are given the opportunity to be true to themselves.

There is a practical side to this also, as there is to everything American. The tendency of industrial enterprise is to wind up into big units in the name of efficiency; but Americans have always been aware of another kind of efficiency, a more creative kind, that can be achieved through decentralization—that is to say, through a diversity of operations. Outsiders often boggle at the idea of competition. But they should remember that competition in America is not the dog-eat-dog affair that social planners and Russian propaganda have made it out to be. Competition has caused suffering in America; it still does hurt when your company is thrown out of business and your job is lost. And yet the essence of American competition is far less desperate than that. It involves the releasing of energies, primarily, for the development of new ideas, new modifications, new "slants," any one of which may end up by revolutionizing some segment of human affairs. That is what diversity means to an American. And that is why he welcomes the existence in his society of people, of beliefs, of ideas that are difficult if not impossible to reconcile.

Thus it will be found upon closer inspection that there is not just one American way of life. There are American *ways* of life, almost without number. For example, there are the great regional differentiations, where nature herself has conspired with American institutions to create ways of life as different from each other as those of two nations might be. It is true that these American "subnations" are bound together by many common ties, including the important tie of language; yet their temperamental characteristics, their customs, their values and views, their personal objectives differ so greatly that a man who is happy and effective in one might be miserable and frustrated in another.

Take the Far West. This vast area, which begins, roughly speaking, at the eastern border of Colorado, has of course many things in common with the rest of the U.S. Yet the ways of those people are very different from the ways of the Easterner. Nature herself has made sure of that, for the Far West is a region of majestic drama, of mountains and buttes and deserts, beside which the woods and streams of the east coast look puny. The western people, generally speaking, are more outspoken than the Easterners, more cordial, more generous of their time and money; they speak slower, and they have a way of cutting through a lot of argument to reach a quick conclusion on which they are willing to stand or fall. The Easterner is endlessly fascinated by them; but he considers them naive, unsophisticated, lacking in perspective in the ways of the world. In fact, the West is to the East as the East is to Europe.

And yet, as anyone knows who has lived out there, these generalizations misrepresent the realities. The Far West itself includes many ways of life. Take, for example, the differences between the Pacific Northwest and California. In the Pacific Northwest the great rivers rise in snow-capped mountains and wind down through gorges to the sea. The cities are incredibly young— Seattle has not yet celebrated its centenary. It is trade-union country and the standard of living is high. But happiness is pursued in the Northwest with a certain calm simplicity that is rare in America. For all the youth of his region, the Northwesterner is something of a philosopher; he expects a lot out of life, but he doesn't aim to get very rich. He attends to his business all right, but he is more interested in his mountains and his waters; he would rather pack up with his wife and kids, with about $200 worth of camping gear in the back of his car, and push off for a ten-day tour of his magnificent state parks; or go cruising in a small boat, or salmon fishing in the foaming streams of the Columbia River watershed, or skiing on the mighty slopes of Mount Rainier.

In the eyes of the Northwesterner, the Californian, therefore, is a noisy fellow. The Californian goes about in bright informal clothing of many colors and lolls on bright beaches along the shores of the bright-blue Pacific and grows oranges that shine brightly from the dark-green foliage of the orange trees. That is to say, the southern Californian does; the northern Californian is altogether different. Northern California merges with the Pacific Northwest and has its roots firmly planted in San Francisco, the westernmost metropolis of Western civilization. San Francisco has become a place where a man can find anything he wants to find, which is perhaps the best definition of metropolitanism.

But Los Angeles, which is the headquarters of the southern Californian, is not like that. Los Angeles is big and boastful and overrun with Easterners and movie actors and cultists of infinite variety. It is also the mecca of the retired couple who took the life-insurance ads seriously and have come out here to enjoy "beauty" and "leisure" and watch the sun set westwardly over the Pacific. But the Northwesterner has the feeling, as he passes the innumerable little "bungalows" that sprawl out into what was only a few decades ago a near desert, that the beauty is wasted here, that it is not appreciated as in the Northwest, that it has not been absorbed. Somehow, like the movie industry that it houses, southern California seems to be removed one step from the real, to live in a world that nature never made—or, for that matter, man. That is the big difference between southern California and the Northwest.

Then there is that other vast region of the U.S., lying between the Rocky Mountains and the Appalachians, where a river may be a thousand miles long, and where everything drains into the Mississippi. Here all lines are horizontal, life is intensely practical and "real," and the quarter-sections and the fields and the towns duplicate themselves, league after league, in seemingly endless repetition. It is here in this great "valley" that the itinerant lecturer has his worst time and reaches his most pessimistic conclusions; for unless these people are studied community by community, they appear to vanish into sociological generalizations.

But actually when you come to know Kansas you find it very different from Minnesota, for example, with its high percentage of Swedes and Germans and a better-balanced economy than Kansas has ever had. Kansas, Nebraska, and the Dakotas are heavy agricultural exporters; their way of life is based upon the soil, and even their towns exist for the farmers, not the towns-people. This makes town life quite different from that of an eastern town, or even of a town in a manufacturing area of the Midwest (such as Chicago or St. Louis, for example), where the town exists, so to speak, for itself, and lives on its own exports. The Midwest farmer is fat with the world's riches—and safe from its depredations. But he is not in the least soft. On the contrary, he has time after time challenged the power of the East, which he regards with a congenital suspicion that is much more marked in the Midwest than in the Far West.

The Midwest merges into the South, and as it does the standard of living declines. The South is problem country. It grew up differently from the rest of the nation, with an economy based on big landholdings and slave labor. It still has with it the problem of the Negro; in many towns of Mississippi and Alabama the Negroes outnumber the whites, who cling to their political power by any means, fair or foul. The Southern way of life differs radically from other American ways of life. The pace is slower. The extremes of poverty and riches are greater. The traditions are better preserved. The storied Southern "aristocracy" is becoming something of a myth, but it has left behind it the tradition of Southern cooking, which is supposed to be the best in the U.S. (though no vestige of it is to be found in the hotels and public eating places); of hospitality, which makes the New Yorker look like a boor; of flirtatious women; and of peaceful ways whose like is to be found nowhere else in the U.S.

And then there is Texas, the independent nation that became a state in 1845. Geographically Texas belongs to both the Midwest and the South, but in terms of its way of life it belongs to neither. Maybe California has outstripped Texas in population growth, but Texas has got richer faster than any comparable region of the U.S. ever has. Oil derricks, skyscrapers, flamboyant hotels, oil and gas pipelines, canals, piers, and great industrial shapes have sprung like mushrooms from a landscape that the Northwesterner would consider quite drab. It is the land of the big rich; the making of wealth dominates the way of life. And yet wealth is really only a symbol for the Texan; he likes to spend it just as wildly as he makes it; he loves the "feel" of struggle, the exhilaration of victory, of "getting ahead." Everything here is on a big scale, as if the gods had lifted the curtain for a drama in Valhalla. The young folks associate in droves—one of their barbecues will be attended by a hundred or more. As an Easterner once complained, he wished that Texans could be friendly on a neighborhood basis instead of on a state basis. The ordinary Texan thinks nothing of driving two or three hundred miles just to see a "local" football game.

The Texan way of life, indeed, represents an extension into the twentieth century of certain ideas that animated all Americans up to the First World War. Here is the land of opportunity, where anybody can rise to the "top," where tomorrow is unpredictable and yesterday unnecessary. Here the intrepid individual, the risk, the adventure, the fabulous reward, have somehow come to fruition in a world largely occupied with the less romantic problems of social "security" and social "science." It is possible for the modern American to feel somewhat nostalgic about Texas, however he may smile—or cringe— at its excesses.

But in the East the way of life is crowded. In the winter the Easterner takes to the trains and planes if he wants to go anywhere; in the summer he chugs despondently along obsolete highways, breathing carbon monoxide from the car ahead, snarled in the traffic of his innumerable cities. He lives in an industrial jungle. His most awe-inspiring sights are not the works of nature but the works of man. He is caught in a maze of brick walls and steel shapes, communication lines and enormous switchboards, six-lane clover-leaf highways and railroad switchyards of such complexity that the eye cannot predict

15

the path that a train will follow through them. The island of Manhattan consists of only twenty-two square miles of rocky land; but two million people live on it, tier above tier, with the subways and three trunk-line railroads underneath them, and tunnels under the subways, and tunnels under the rivers, and eighteen bridges gripping Long Island and the mainland. And all around them are clustered miles on miles of houses, and highways extending outward to the "dormitory towns." The Westerner could not endure it.

Yet the East is exciting, too. It generates ideas—big, continental ideas that have had enormous influence in the development of America. The ideas radiate outward and merge with native ideas in the different regions, to bring forth new ventures and new shapes. Thus from the Manhattan apex there extends westward an enormous triangle, one side 900 miles to Chicago, the other 1,000 miles to St. Louis. This is the "industrial triangle," the jugular vein of Western civilization. If an enemy could knock it out, or any substantial part of it, the U.S. would be unable to fight. For it contains more than half of all the capital investment of American industry and employs more than half of the industrial workers. Yet even within the triangle the ways of life differ. The people of Pittsburgh, who live among the ruddy fires of the steel mills, are "Westerners" to the New Yorker, who works or lives several hundred feet above the earth, has two martinis for lunch, and charges the rest of the country exorbitant sums for the use of his fertile imagination. And the people of Chicago really belong to the Midwest.

16

Nor is the way of life in New York City the same as the way of life in Boston, the hub of another industrial complex, composed chiefly of textiles, machine tools, high skills, and industrial specialties. Perhaps New England contains more incongruities than any region. The "elite"—for here, at any rate, there are such—still cling to a great cultural tradition that reached its climax with Ralph Waldo Emerson and shed a mellow light into the twentieth century through the pen of Henry Adams. Boston still has in the Athenaeum the nation's most notable private library, whose shelves are accessible only to "proprietors"; and it also has in the Widener at Harvard the biggest university library in the world. Yet the casual visitor to New England, including the American tourist who goes there for his summer vacation, has increasing difficulty in finding vestiges of the cultural tradition; for a large part of New England is encased like one of its famous clams in a shell of modern industrialization in all of its ugliest aspects, including a plethora of billboards and hot-dog stands, together with an ex-Governor recently released from jail.

It is commonly said that the ruggedness for which New England was once famed is on the wane. Yet this is not really the case, as anyone who tries to live there will soon discover. Up in Vermont and New Hampshire you will find a stubborn folk who have never yielded to the most "advanced" versions of the industrialized life—in a number of instances they have even refused to accept federal aid. And even in the industrialized sections you will find plenty of individuals who live in the fear of God and the love of competition. Within its industrialized

17

shell the New England clam still flourishes—sober, hard-working, inventive, prudent, much more reserved than the Westerner, and downright unsympathetic to the flashy airs of the California goldfish.

Which one of these ways of life does the American mean by "the American way of life"? The answer is none of them. New England is no more "American" than the Northwest, nor Denver more so than Atlanta. This diversity itself is the way of life—nations within a nation.

Nor can the way of life be defined by the life of any one particular community—the late Sinclair Lewis notwithstanding. For it is at the community level that America really begins to get diverse, because American life is not regional but local. The life of one town is influenced by a newspaper editor who wrote a history of his county and is a specialist on Indian warfare; the life of another, by a doctor interested in psychology. Here is a town addicted to schottisches, another whose social life centers around a Norwegian Harmony Club, another that features Czech gymnastic festivals. Here is a town with a Chinese restaurant; over there a town with German *verein;* over there a town, redolent of frijoles, that speaks mostly Spanish. All cultures are cherished—interwoven—modified. Here there are no memories and the town is flat and everyone eats out of cans. But there the memories of the old country are strong; the housewives treasure old Finnish recipes handed down from grandmothers who never saw America; or creole dishes, or Irish remedies for the gout.

And all this is accented by the extremists, the indi-

vidualists, the eccentrics: the man with a thousand ca-
naries; the man who keeps five buffalo in Connecticut;
the electrician with odd working hours who spends his
mornings in the town library in blue jeans reading Shakespeare; the nudists, the vegetarians, the Indian fortune-
tellers, the perpetual-motion inventors; the Amish who
won't wear buttons; the old lady who writes poetry in
the manner of Sara Teasdale. And then there are the
hobbyists—the carpenters and gardeners—the man in the
Great Plains who builds model ships—the amateur paint-
ers—the man who plays the flute in the morning—the
expert on Japanese prints—the collector of chess sets.
The way of life is none of these ways of life. And as for
"standardization," it is lost in a forest of human foibles.

And yet, also, the way of life is *all* of these. For there
is an extraordinary unity in this diversity, a coherence
that resists all eccentricities, all power concentrations
even. And this unity, which is not merely national in
the ordinary sense of the word, pertains to quite another
level of existence, another level of values from that which
manifests itself with such diversity. It has to do with
ideals, with a complex of principles and beliefs, to which
all American life has reference. The truth, which has
thus far been difficult for the rest of the world to grasp,
is that Americans live on two planes at once—the practical and the ideal. The conflicts created by this ambivalent existence, which worry other people so much that
they often feel constrained to reject one plane or the
other, bother the American scarcely at all. Take for example one of his leading national characteristics.

"I wish to preach," said Theodore Roosevelt at the turn of the century, "not the doctrine of ignoble ease, but the doctrine of the strenuous life." And when he said that he said something profoundly American. The strenuosity of American life simply appalls the European. Why go at things so hard? Why take these interminable gambles, follow these restive hunches, constantly uproot that which has been successfully established? Why not be content with that which is good enough?

Of course, lots of things have happened since T. R. made that remark. In terms of physical work—of *toil*—American life is far less strenuous. The forty-hour week is almost universal; Saturdays are for the most part holidays; the lunch break is getting longer. The ECA productivity teams that visited this country observed that Americans did not seem to work any harder than Europeans. However, they got more done, and that is perhaps the key to the matter. Increasingly, Americans are emphasizing *mind*. They have discovered that through the use of the mind, especially in the development of technology, life can be made strenuous in a different and pleasanter way. To the visitor, whose technology may not be so advanced, or whose powers of invention may be less well developed, the distinction may seem somewhat academic; American life remains too strenuous to emulate. But to the American the distinction is a real one. He has discovered ways to keep up the pace without the physical punishment that old T. R. very likely had in mind. What makes his modern life strenuous, therefore, is simply that he insists *that the pace be kept up.*

The outsider, to be sure, may wonder to what purpose. For Americans not only work hard, they play hard; simple gaiety, as the Italians know it, for example, seems not to be in their make-up. All the energy that the American saves from toil by the smart application of technology is freely expended on his most conspicuous passion, the great American outdoors. In every section of the country, even the industrial East, Americans pour out an incredible amount of energy whacking golf balls, playing tennis and baseball, hiking, camping, sailing, fishing, hunting—everything but just "walking." Most foreigners fail to understand—let alone enjoy—all this dashing around. The strenuous life is bad enough at the factory: why double it during leisure time? This reaction is a matter of temperament, and Americans must be prepared to accept the criticism that they are just too damn energetic.

However, there is a principle involved which foreigners ought not to overlook. In the view of the American, life is not just a matter of the conservation of energy. On the contrary, in his experience, energy creates energy; a good hard game of tennis, or a hike in the hills, will actually improve your mental faculties the next morning. Thus the pace of technological life is maintained, not through the cultivation of repose, but by building up a kind of counterforce through physical exertions—supported, to be sure, by abundant vitamins. Here is *mens sana in corpore sano*, but raised to a higher power—to the great advantage, incidentally, of the seven-billion-dollar sports and vacation industries.

21

The strenuous life, then, is an American characteristic. But it is interesting, not merely as a characteristic, but because it illustrates so aptly the ambivalent nature of the American. The strenuous life derives, on the one hand, from the practical necessities of a virginal continent on which there was much work to do. But it derives, on the other, from an *ideal:* the ideal of the perfectibility of man, of human improvement. Where this ideal came from is a matter for scholars to debate; it has in any case been accepted in one form or another by Americans from the very beginning. It has given rise to many American faults, such as over-optimism and a superficial concept of "progress." But above all, it has kept Americans working, risking, venturing, striving; it has sparked the strenuous life.

This same ambivalence manifests itself in many other American characteristics. For instance, take those characteristics having to do with the great ideal of Equality, the fundamental "tendency" of American life, as shown in "The American System" (Chapter III). The confidence that he is the equal of any man gives the American a certain ease of manner, even a brashness, which can be extremely irritating to those who have not been bred to "equality." On the other hand, it helps the American to be a friendly fellow, a trait that almost every foreigner notices upon arriving on our shores— despite the seemingly deliberate inhospitality of the immigration service and the customs officials. The American does not recognize many social barriers. This is especially true of the West, where the man who is painting your house will probably call you by your first name before you have decided how to address him. One of the little shockers for American labor leaders who went to England some while ago to help with productivity was the sight of English workers tipping their hats to the boss. American workers consider themselves the equals of the boss in everything except the externals, so they don't tip their hats. In fact—and this is the key to an understanding of Americans—the boss wouldn't like it if they did; it would make him feel uncomfortable: for he too has the ideal of equality.

Equality thus has its positive side: it does not merely equate privileges, it asserts obligations. There is the other fellow, and he has just the same rights as you. This doesn't mean that Americans go around thinking of the "other fellow" all the time; in fact, they may be planning some competitive scheme to put him out of business. But they are oriented from their childhood to the idea of the rights of other people. The civil liberties are not merely constraining laws. They, too, are ideals, imperfectly realized, but entering into the life of every American in such a way as to encourage qualities or virtues, the best word for which is "democratic."

The American has an ideal of generosity, also. He doesn't live up to this one any better than—or even as well as—he lives up to the related ideals of the civil liberties; but generosity is bred into him, nevertheless, as a great democratic virtue. Sometimes the American's generosity is no more than an openhanded way of doing things, which at its worst leads to sheer waste. At its best, however, no other national characteristic exhibits more clearly the way the American can combine the ideal and the practical. For, aside from its ethical status, generosity appeals to the American as an eminently practical trait to encourage. Wouldn't it be a much better world if everybody were generous? Then nobody, including you yourself, would have to worry so much. That is the practical side of the matter. But, he would add, you should never carry it so far as to look like a "sucker."

Still another ideal related to the general ideal of equality is that of kindness. This too the American regards as a democratic virtue. The American is capable of being brutish and some people think of him as ruthless. He himself likes to parade as a "tough guy." But his armor is usually paper-thin, and there are apt to be vulnerable spots—for example, children. Americans love children to the point of being silly about them, as almost everyone who has known the G.I.'s has observed. In fact, they universally spoil their own.

Whether Americans have more or less of these democratic virtues, whether they are friendlier than other people, or more generous, or kinder, is not at all the point. Such generalizations can never be proved and only lead to resentful arguments. The point is that Americans, practical and pragmatic by temperament, have nevertheless taken very seriously certain ideals having to do in a general way with the ideal of democratic equality.

And perhaps, next to their Proposition itself, this is the most valuable contribution that Americans have to offer the world. It is wrong, at the present stage of our evolution, to expect some great "cultural" development in America, equivalent to the culture of Europe that extends back for twenty or twenty-five creative centuries. The intellectuals who castigate Americans on this score miss the point. In the first place, they overlook the fact that there is a great activity in the creative arts throughout the country, especially at the community level; and second, they too easily forget that American culture is of necessity a *popular* culture, and hence inherently different from that which we inherit from Europe. Yet even after these modifications have been made, the fact remains that high culture is not what Americans have primarily to give. The big American contribution to Western civilization has to do, rather, with certain qualities of the heart deriving from democratic ideals. These ideals, in the form of recognized democratic virtues, are constantly at work in American society, and have a great deal to do with what is meant by "the American way of life." In fact, if this were not so, if the ideals were to vanish, or if Americans were to abandon the hope that people would someday learn to practice them, then the American way of life, as Americans construe it today, would also disappear. It would become something quite different. It survives as it is only on the presumption that most of the people will try to realize the democratic virtues most of the time.

Yet these ideals that the American cherishes are not just hung up in the air. They have a reference point that walks and talks and is "real"—the individual human being. Everything in America, be it national, regional, subregional, or local, comes back somehow to the individual. And the American can live his life on two planes at once in such a strenuous way precisely because he recognizes that the human individual may have—must have—ideals. That is the inner secret of the American way of life. It is a way of life to permit and encourage the development of the human individual, by his own free will, toward his own ideals.

This fact is nowhere better illustrated than in the American attitude toward "standardization." To see "standardization" as the American sees it, one must bring it back to the individual. The intelligent American will agree that standardization represents a certain danger. But on the other hand he will point out that in his society —in the American way of life—the individual does have opportunity, does develop and grow. And in the light of this great, essential truth he can put standardization in a certain perspective, which Europeans have not yet learned. For what is being standardized in America? Not the individual human spirit, which the American way of life intends to hold inviolately free. But the things that the human spirit uses—these are being standardized: the houses and vehicles, the tools and machines, to some extent the clothing and even the food. But these are, after all, the shell. They are not the human being himself, and so long as American institutions are careful to distinguish between human beings and things, why not standardize the things? Nature herself, after all, has in a certain sense standardized the human body. We don't expect to find people with five arms or with eyes in the backs of their heads. But we don't say for that reason that the human spirit cannot be free. The body is just a vehicle.

Indeed, to say that standardization must be the death of freedom is to express a far more materialistic attitude than the American attitude. It is to define man in terms of things—in terms of his body. To the American, his machines and gadgets are *extensions* of man. They are extensions of his faculties and powers—wings to enable him to fly, wheels to enable him to run, antennae to enable him to hear and see at great distances. Americans, indeed, have taken on the task of extending man in this way with a certain positive attitude, as if it were their special cosmic assignment. They really believe and really feel that they are doing something important, not to enchain the human soul, but to increase its power and scope, and thus to help emancipate it from the merely physical, from the earth. That is the positive side of American "materialism."

As for "conformity," the danger here may be greater, because one is not dealing with things but with the standardization of people themselves. Yet here too the same principle can be applied to a certain extent. Much American conformity may be due to a kind of social compulsion that is highly undesirable; but much of it also is simply a matter of convenience. The reason why garden clubs are more or less alike is not that anyone compels them to be alike, but just because it is easier to organize them that way. Anyone who might try to *enforce* conformity upon an American would find out soon enough that where his convictions are concerned he is capable of non-conformity to the point of bloodshed. Here, too,

27

the American feels, a little perspective is in order. Conformity has not yet engulfed him. And he doubts that it ever really will.

This central focus of the American way of life—the concept of the inviolability of the human individual—was born politically in the Age of Reason and implemented by the announcement of the American Proposition, as set forth in the next chapter. But spiritually, of course, this concept goes back to the founding of Christianity, whence the American derives his basic ideal of the individual. Christianity has had many versions in America, many strange and eccentric variants. Yet it has always been inherent in the American way of life, binding it together in subtle ways, even for Americans who do not actually profess it. The idea of the perfectibility of man, for example, which gives Americans so much drive, is a Christian ideal. And the democratic virtues, which have to do with the relation of one man to another, are essentially Christian virtues. The American's Christianity is, to be sure, somewhat one-sided; his idea of "perfectibility," for example, is theologically naive; his optimism leads him to overlook some of the profounder, more tragic depths of the human soul; he is apt to translate spiritual truths too facilely into practical terms. Nevertheless, his tremendous faith in the human spirit saves him, most of the time, from the consequences of his own errors—and may yet save the free world.

For the forces released by this faith are dynamic, in the sense that there is no point at which their action may be calculated to cease. It is impossible to talk about the

28

American way of life without talking about change. Twenty-one years ago, when FORTUNE was founded, the present volume could not have been written: for the face of America twenty-one years ago, and during the stormy period of the thirties, was the face of a society that could not solve, did not know how to solve, internal problems that threatened to destroy it. To take the matter of industrial relations alone, violence, espionage, and coercion were commonplace. The right to organize and bargain collectively, which in an industrial society is a minimum social right, was recognized in theory but was little practiced. Bloodshed and hate stalked the streets of Gadsden, Toledo, Detroit, Aliquippa. Looking back, indeed, these memories seem almost incredible: not because we have solved all of our internal problems, but because industrial violence, at least, is now recognized as a social crime. There is growing up in our society, as pointed out in "Individualism Comes of Age" (Chapter XI), a sense of social partnership that only the craziest optimist could have predicted from the social data of the thirties.

In his speeches before the United Nations, Mr. Vishinsky has sought to portray Americans in terms of their own past—blacker than their past ever was, to be sure, but nevertheless reminiscent of problems they used to have. That is deliberate misrepresentation and it makes the American mad. But what makes him even madder is that this constitutes an attempt to *fix him in time*, to arrest him in the image, however caricatured, of what he used to be. And, on top of his anger, the American is then chagrined to find that other people, people whom he considers to be his friends and allies, half believe what Mr.

Vishinsky says; are indeed so blind to the native dynamism within the American way of life, released by the energies of free individuals, that they fail to take into account the constant change, the constant correction of errors, the constant reappraisal, the constant evolution of American aims. Americans wish that other people could see their country as it really is: not as an achievement, but as a *process*—a process of becoming.

What the purpose of the "becoming" is, and where it leads to, are not yet questions for the American way of life. Perhaps the day will come when this kind of question will occupy Americans, but thus far their mission has been the mission of action—the mission of the will. Metaphysical speculation is hardly yet a national specialty. In the American's eyes the individual is, in the end, an enigma. Therefore, America is an enigma.

Anyone inclined to doubt that America is an enigma should study the Great Seal, reproduced on every dollar bill: an Egyptian pyramid rising from a mysterious plain; a mystic eye blazing light from the pyramid's tip; and an occult inscription, "*Annuit Coeptis . . . Novus ordo seclorum.*" Practically no American can tell you what that seal means. But that is not the point. The point is that the American way of life embodies a mystery, which no one has yet solved, but which is common to all men: the mystery of the human spirit.

This chapter would fit in with a section of the course dealing with institutional capitalism, free enterprise, comparative economic systems (as far as motivation is concerned), socio-economic background for our economic system, etc. It has strong emphasis on individualism, dynamism, the urge to be diverse, always changing, democratic idealism, what makes the U.S. diverse in peoples and geography yet bound together.

THE AMERICAN PROPOSITION

THE "AMERICAN WAY OF LIFE," then, is a phrase that must be read in two different ways. On the one hand it refers to a vast and complex network of human particulars which have developed on American soil and which characterize American society. These particulars are, so to speak, non-transferable: they cannot be imagined as native to any other society on earth. But on the other hand, the "American Way of Life" is animated by certain ideals. This fact in itself is not peculiar: the British way of life, the French way of life, the Belgian way of life, and so forth, are also animated by ideals. But the peculiarity of the American ideals is to be found in the attitude that Americans entertain toward them. To a large extent the American ideals replace (and often conflict with) the conventional concept of nationality. The American, in short, takes them to be human

31

ideals—universals belonging to all mankind, of which he is in certain respects the custodian.

This notion of custodianship can be profoundly irritating to other people, who do not see why Americans should consider themselves specially appointed to such a task, and who are quick to point out that they are not in any case doing it very well. Yet for the American, the idea of custodianship has deep roots in his own history. The history of the U.S.A. begins with a revolution. And the merest glance at the fundamental documents of the time shows that, in the eyes of its leaders, it was not merely a revolution against Britain but a revolution in human affairs. It had, indeed, been in preparation for many hundreds of years; but the opportunity to realize it came in eighteenth-century America, and it has been carried on ever since. It was—and is—the revolution of the human individual against all forms of enslavement; against all forms of earthly power, whether spiritual, political, or economic, that seek to govern man without consulting his individual will. Inherent to it was—and is—a proposition. We call this the American Proposition, inasmuch as it is to be found most succinctly stated in the writings and speeches of the founders of this country. But in the eyes of those founders it was not merely a proposition for Americans; it was universal: a proposition for mankind, signalizing not merely an American revolution but a human revolution.

The universal relevance of the American Proposition has been asserted again and again by American leaders; and so has its corollary, that America itself—that "grand scheme and design in Providence," as John Adams called it—has a mission to present the Proposition to the rest of the world. Liberty and self-government, said George Washington, are "*finally* staked on the experiment entrusted to the hands of the American people." Lincoln called our revolution "the germ which has vegetated, and still is to grow and expand into the universal liberty of mankind." Wilson said we were "destined to set a responsible example to all the world of what free government is and can do"; nor was he the first or last President to try to express that sense of mission in a missionary diplomacy. Said Emerson, "The Office of America is to liberate."

Since America was born and brought up with this sense of its own universal import, this generation of Americans has a duty either to renounce it or reaffirm it in a way that is clear both to ourselves and to mankind. The editors of FORTUNE wish to reaffirm the Proposition—not as an academic exercise in eighteenth-century philosophy, but as it applies to the men and nations of our time. This short chapter, and the longer one immediately following ("The American System"), are attempts to define the American Proposition as we understand it and as we wish to advocate it. First we examine its essence, the sacredness of the free individual and the Rights to be derived therefrom. Next we descend somewhat to the realm of political theory, to show the living principles through which the Proposition has manifested itself in the American system of government. In both cases we have sought to distinguish between what is merely American, and hence transitory, and what is universal and timeless. The Proposition and the System together constitute a single whole.

The essence of the American Proposition can be understood only against the long religious history of mankind that preceded its formulation. Man first discovered the fatherhood of God, then the brotherhood of all men in Christ; and as he grew in spiritual understanding, he was released in the custody of his own conscience, to seek good and shun evil according to his own lights. This spiritual freedom is real because man was created by God in the "image" of God. Man carries within him something that the merely animal does not have, the divine spark, the "image." Since every man is thus *of* God, every man is *equal,* in the sense that no man can claim he is more important to God than any other man. The human individual thus has a special status with regard to all other things and beings on earth: he must live, and must be entitled to live, by the laws of God, not just by the laws and directives of men.

According to the American Proposition, this special status of the individual is couched in certain Rights with which everyone is endowed. It is specifically stated in the Declaration of Independence that man is endowed with these Rights *by his Creator;* the Rights, therefore, are not man-made but God-made. They are "unalienable," grounded in the universe itself, reflecting universal laws of nature: that is to say, they are natural, not merely political, Rights. The human individual is clothed with them and no other man or group of men is entitled by God's law to strip them from him.

The three natural Rights mentioned in the Declaration of Independence are Life, Liberty, and the Pursuit of Happiness. We are told that these three are only "among others," but in fact no other Right of equal rank has been formulated. The founders' language is at once so broad and so well chosen that all the *civil* rights necessary to the maintenance of freedom can logically be derived from the three *natural* Rights that the Proposition names.

These natural Rights have not been mere theories in America. They have lived in the hearts of the people. They actuated the Revolutionary War, the Civil War, and much thereafter. Indeed, the thesis can be sustained that in the last analysis American history has been a struggle to define and implement these Rights, and that this struggle is still going on. The great social issues of our time, for example, can be construed as attempts to redefine the Right to Life in terms of an industrialized society. From the Right to Liberty, on the other hand, there spring all the *political* safeguards that Americans have erected to protect the individual. And the Right to the Pursuit of Happiness, if as yet less well defined, opens up for the individual the opportunity to develop himself according to his own cultural and spiritual lights.

Many Americans feel uncomfortable about restating an eighteenth-century proposition in so different a century, feeling that these ideas may in fact be dead, or if not dead obsolete, or if not obsolete doomed. And, indeed, there are many dangers involved in this course. There is the danger, in the first place, of using the great thoughts of the founding fathers as a substitute for our own thoughts, and of inviting the development, in a time of trouble, of a kind of nationalistic religion complete with dusty relics and inviolate dogma. There is the danger— not unallied with this—of feeding the fire of our native optimism by throwing upon it the more respectable but no less inflammable optimism of the eighteenth century, with its innocent belief in the goodness of man and the automatism of progress. And there is, if not the danger, then the difficulty of dealing with our modern pragmat- ism, which contends that it is unnecessary to dabble in the transcendental, or, except in a "subjective" way, in questions pertaining to the divine.

We acknowledge these dangers and difficulties, and we face some of them in the pages of this book. But we suggest also that many of them are met, in fact or by inference, in the title we have chosen for this book: the *permanent* revolution. This phrase was invented by Marx and brought to prominence by Leon Trotsky. But that need not deter us. The entire Bolshevik revolution, it is now clear, was just another counter-revolution against liberty—the biggest, perhaps, but still one of many. Moreover, to call any Communist revolution "per- manent" is a contradiction in terms. A social and political revolution takes place against something: if it fails, it disappears; if it succeeds, it replaces the status quo against which it rebelled and becomes itself the status quo. The contradiction in Trotsky's use of the phrase is thus revealed by a simple question: should the Com- munist revolution succeed totally, what would be left for it to rebel against? The answer is, nothing. The completion of that "revolution" would impose upon mankind a total and permanent tyranny.

This is not the case with the American revolution. The revolution of the individual can never become the status quo, because the human spirit, as revealed in Palestine by the founder of Christianity, is limitless. Therefore the task of the revolution, which is to make that spirit free on earth, can never be finished. We cannot say at any given point, here we are free. We can say only that with reference to the past we have gained some degree or some fragment of freedom. We have gained free speech, however imperfectly; but what about the thinking behind the speech, which gives purpose to it? Are we not still chained in our thinking to prejudice and ignorance? Are we not still the slaves of error?

The individual lives surrounded by darkness. He is a mere candle. The task of the permanent revolution is to increase the light of that candle, the light of every candle, so that one light may reach to another light and the darkness may thus be dispelled. Here in this land, by learning to apply the Proposition, we have gained some elementary steps. We have gained in the first place the principle that every candle has a right to shine. That is the political right. We have made extraordinary progress in the direction of providing every candle with the material fuel that it needs. That is the economic right. Yet in pursuit of real freedom we have yet to gain much more than we have won. We have not begun to gain freedom from error, the freedom that comes from right reason. We have not begun to gain freedom from hate, the freedom that is born of love.

37

This is the meaning of our wars: this is the only meaning that can give them meaning. Yet the truth is, we cannot by ourselves reach these higher aspects of freedom; we can reach them only if the Proposition is accepted as universal and if we can learn to share it with other peoples of the earth. For it belongs to all mankind.

This chapter has more to commend it in the field of political philosophy and theory than in economics. In general, the American Proposition as a re-statement of elements of natural law as embodied in the Constitution in "life, liberty and the pursuit of happiness."

iii

THE AMERICAN SYSTEM

HAVING DECLARED THEIR BELIEF in the natural rights of the individual, and thus laid down the universal essence of the American Proposition, our eighteenth-century Founding Fathers next faced the practical consequences of this bold stand: how harmonize these rights with the fact that man, even if sacred, is also a social and political animal? It is one thing to declare Rights that practically everybody would like to possess; it is quite another to prove that you know a better way to "secure these rights" than the government you are overthrowing. Any and all governments are what Tom Paine called them: "like dress . . . the badge of lost innocence"; and therefore the very science of government, let alone its various working models, is bound to have some kind of human imperfection in it. The founders knew this well; but they also felt they could improve not only on the

39

British government of George III, but on all governments previously known to history. Moreover, they were right.

This is a large statement. It might have been taken for granted a generation or two ago, when a certain amount of idolatry of our Founding Fathers was fashionable. It can be sustained today without idolatry. The Founding Fathers were great and talented men of very high I.Q. who happened to face an unparalleled historical opportunity and made the most of it. They did so by deliberately mastering everything that was knowable in their time about the branch of learning most relevant to their problem, namely, political philosophy. They came out of their quest knowing more about this subject, and knowing that they knew more, than any men of their time. They were repeatedly appalled at the comparative political ignorance of their European friends, from Condorcet to Turgot. Whatever political science had to teach, the founders learned it.

Moreover, they were able to apply their learning to an almost virgin society. Ours was "the best opportunity," John Adams said, "and the greatest trust . . . that Providence ever committed to so small a number since the transgression of the first pair." The result of this happy coincidence was a political system whose essential principles are still wholly distinguishable from the society it governs. In no other civilized country is this distinction so clear. Even in England, whose constitution has many common origins with ours, the cauldron of time has so blended the way of life and the political system that the liberties of Englishmen probably owe more to the character of Englishmen than to the English system. The American Way of Life is the product of time, but the essential principles of the American political system are not. They have survived the cauldron but owe nothing to it. They were adopted for our country at a certain time by certain men, and everything important that has since happened to our political system was allowed for, even in part foreseen, by its creators.

This claim would be extravagant if it could not be supported by another—namely, that political philosophy has made absolutely no progress in its essentials from the time when Adams, Jefferson, Hamilton, and Madison were its world masters to the present. It will therefore be found, as we examine it, that the political system they created still exhibits certain truths which are applicable now as then to the government of any people or "way of life" under the sun.

The essential principles of the American political system are very simple. They are three: a word, a tendency, and a method. The word is liberty. The tendency is equality. The method is constitutionalism.

Constitutionalism is not the same thing as the Constitution. Constitutionalism, also sometimes called "pluralism" or "the principle of limitation," is a general name for a mechanical contraption of which almost every generation of Americans has brought forth a new model. Among these models have been checks and balances, states' rights, balance of power, concurrent majority, sectionalism, trust-busting, civil service, decentralization, "the TVA idea," what not. The unchanging purpose

41

served by this changing machine is the negative one of keeping the power of the central government out of the hands of any one group of people whose common interest, whether economic, sectional, or ideological, might prove too strong for the liberties of the rest. Constitutionalism expresses the conviction that all governments are a potential menace to liberty.

Thus there is a direct link between liberty and constitutionalism. But liberty and equality are also linked. In the eighteenth century their interdependence was considered so obvious that some Jeffersonians would trust freedom only to the self-sufficient members of a "gopher democracy," small farmers neither rich enough to corrupt nor poor enough to be corrupted by the central government. When this connection became less obvious in the nineteenth century, Abraham Lincoln made it clear for his time at least by reminding us, "Those who deny freedom to others deserve it not for themselves, and under a just God will not long retain it."

There is also a connection between equality and constitutionalism. This accommodating method gives victims of inequality a way to redress their wrongs or vent their feelings without being tempted to take over the government forever. Under it, every man can be a "king" if he has to—but only for a limited period or in a limited area (Huey Long's Louisiana). At the same time constitutionalism permits experiments in equality that, as Bryce noted, "could not safely be made in a large centralized country," but can be adopted nationally when their trial period is over.

Thus each of the three ingredients in the American

system is linked with the other two, the triad forming a circle. Yet not a closed circle, for the society it frames is not a closed society. There are little gaps. It is open not only to accommodate social change and the necessities of national survival, but to leave room for one ultimate mystery, the mystery of man's nature. This mystery, on the answer to which the Founding Fathers held some-what diverse ideas, caused them to refer repeatedly to the American system as an experiment. America was and is a laboratory test of the age-old problem that makes political philosophy a branch of moral philosophy: whether (in Jefferson's words) "men may be trusted to govern themselves without a master," or whether they must be forced to be moral, or even (in Rousseau's phrase) "forced to be free." That question is still open. The founders did not prejudge the moral answer. What they agreed on, however, was a political answer that has kept the experiment going strong and may keep it going forever.

If we examine in turn the word, the tendency, and the method of the American system, we will see more clearly their links with each other and also with the Declaration of Independence and the Constitution.

First the word, liberty. Somebody is always redefining it. Except in moral terms, it is not hard to maintain that it has no meaning at all. Thus it can be argued that he is free who feels himself free, that this feeling is excited by different circumstances in different people or at different times, that it can be excited by a clever dictator. To some Hegelians like Troeltsch, "Liberty consists more in duties

43

than in rights," being the "free, conscious, and dutiful dedication of oneself to the whole, as it has been molded by history, state, and nation." Liberty can also be explained away by subdivision, as by historians who trace it to particular privileges won by particular barons or businessmen, or enumerated to a frazzle, as in the endless consecutive fifths that were inevitably added to F.D.R.'s "four freedoms."

To the men who asserted their own and everybody else's right to "life, liberty, and the pursuit of happiness," the word had a particular and a general meaning. Quite particular was the feeling the American colonists began to get after 1760 that they ought to be free of Great Britain. This feeling, according to John Adams, was the real revolution; it moved Congress to open American ports to non-British trade, after which Adams figured the Declaration of Independence was inevitable. On this showing the Declaration, proclaiming liberty a *universal* right, can be called an inspired fig leaf for middle-class colonial rebelliousness. Tory ex-Governor Hutchinson of Massachusetts had no trouble showing it up as such; if its truths were so self-evident, why did they not apply to the more than 100,000 Africans on American shores?

Yet the word *did* have a general meaning to the colonists, a meaning it bears today. Wrote Adams to John Taylor, "Liberty, according to my metaphysics . . . is a self-determining power in an intellectual agent. It implies thought and choice and power." He also called it "a virgin which everyone seeks to deflower." Its enemies were not the British Government only, but a tendency in all governments; yet a tendency not in governments

44

only, but in other human and social forces that only a government could control. Therefore it was necessary to set up a government with ample but restricted powers. And so, to protect themselves from anarchy and foreigners and "to secure the Blessings of Liberty to ourselves and our Posterity," the fifty-five members of the Constitutional Convention did just that.

In the government they created, the priority of liberty had two practical effects. First, it required the formal use of a theory that, coming straight from John Locke, had already been expressed in the Declaration: all governments derive their just powers from the consent of the governed. This consent theory of government, thanks to American, British, and French precept and example, has spread throughout the Western world, so that no respectable country, certainly among the democracies, dares profess any other.

The priority of liberty had a second effect on the Constitution: the Bill of Rights. Here the idea was not to assert a basic principle but to reinforce "certain fences" around liberty "which the governing powers have ever shown a disposition to weaken and remove." Now the Constitution as written in Jefferson's absence gave the government no power to infringe these rights, and since the government was given only enumerated powers, the framers thought a Bill of Rights superfluous. Jefferson and others insisted on spelling them out, with one far-reaching though not unforeseen consequence. The named rights became inextricably involved with the federal judicial system, which, as their particular guardian, found

45

it possible to assume real equality of power with the legislative and executive branches.

This happened when Marshall, Story, and Kent revitalized the old English doctrine of judicial review, a doctrine that the English have "outgrown" (Parliament being theoretically absolute) but that has never been abdicated by our courts, even those most deferent to the legislative will, such as the present Supreme Court. Judicial review has occasionally produced queer distortions in our politics, particularly from 1880 to 1937, when the courts became an "aristocracy of the robe" and turned the due-process clause into a moat around all forms of private property. But this same power to construe rights has forced American judges, whether aristocrats or democrats, to remain in some degree philosophers of justice, since every Bill of Rights case necessarily suggests questions of first principle, questions that keep our affairs in touch with the tenets of the American Proposition. What is the source of these rights the Court is construing? Who guards their guardian? How reconcile them with each other, with the police power, with justice? Such questions continue to arise under the Bill of Rights in ways that the most pragmatic or cynical judge cannot evade. Willy-nilly he finds himself defending or failing to defend the liberty of one or a few men against the states, against the federal government, even against the sovereign people, whom the founders distrusted in this respect as much as they did monarchs.

Indeed, thought John Adams, the people as a whole, unchecked by well-designed institutions, are "the worst conceivable" keepers of their own liberties; "they are no keepers at all." He won an undeserved reputation for Toryism because he took a pessimistic view of human nature. People like his cousin Sam hoped that liberty would be adequately protected by universal education, which would spread "knowledge, virtue, and benevolence" among the whole people. But when that happens, said John, a little testily, "all civil government is then to cease, and the Messiah is to reign." Meanwhile, since we have to have a strong central government, let us make it one "of laws not men." Jefferson, the supposed (but never self-styled) democrat, did not differ with Adams on this point; he was simply more optimistic about the possibilities. Perhaps someday the Messiah *would* reign. Universal liberty was not synonymous with universal virtue, but it was certainly prior to it, for only a free agent is capable of a morally valid choice between evil and good. Hence liberty is the first step on the road to perfectibility, and science and education will help us on the way. "So we shall go on," wrote Jefferson, "puzzled and prospering beyond example in the history of man." What optimist and pessimist agreed on was the absolute priority of liberty, and the need of protecting it against any and all foes.

Once, when John Adams was in Paris, he saw in a foundling hospital fifty babies each less than a week old. He "attentively observed all their countenances" and concluded that never, even "in the streets of Paris or London," had he seen "a greater variety, or more striking inequalities." Thus did he disprove the notion that all men are "created equal." He went further: "Birth and wealth are conferred upon some men as imperiously by nature as genius, strength or beauty." But this did not prevent him from holding as firmly as Jefferson that in one vital respect all men *are* created equal: they are born to equal rights. This was "as indubitable as a moral government in the universe." That is what Adams meant when he signed the Declaration, and what most of his co-signers meant too.

It is easy to find plenty of strictures on democracy in the works of the Founding Fathers. The word had Athenian connotations then (all decisions of state voted on by all the citizens) and was considered a sure invitation to despotism. The founders called themselves republicans, meaning believers in *representative* government; it was not until the 1830's that the word "democracy" even acquired respectable currency. Yet the consent theory meant that the people *as a whole* were sovereign, and the doctrine of equal rights, as some of the founders well knew, would give the government a bias over time toward broader representation—or, in the modern sense of the term, toward more democracy.

They knew, for example, that slavery would have to yield eventually to the doctrine of equal rights if the Constitution was to survive. Said Jefferson, "Since God is in the universe, slavery must vanish." As early as 1820 the Missouri Compromise sounded to him as "a firebell in the night." As the issue developed, the Declaration of Independence, which had lost its fiery prestige in the world after Napoleon disfigured its message, became a living document again for all whose consciences would not tolerate slavery. The slave power was forced to de-

48

clare its principles "unfounded and false," and trimmers (the vanishing Whigs) called them "glittering generalities." No amount of economic interpretation can conceal the fact that the greatest crisis of the Constitution was precipitated by the Declaration of Independence and the issue of equal rights. That, to Calhoun, was a singularly repulsive fact about the northern crusade: the North's self-interest, he said, was *not* involved; it was forcing the crisis from a conviction of "highest duty."

Yet the Constitution survived this test of its own first principles, as it has survived many lesser tests before and since. It survived the Jeffersonian "revolution," the Jacksonian, that of the long period of judicial oligarchy and populist "revolt," the reforms of T.R., the income tax, the direct election of Senators, women's suffrage, at least five major controversies over the nature of the dollar, the New Freedom, prohibition, and the New Deal. In all these crises the equality of rights, backed by popular sovereignty, was at least implicitly ranged against the rights of the individual. When the latter right was chiefly a property right, equality usually won the eventual compromise. When a more abstract right was disputed, as in prohibition, the individual eventually won; and the most remarkable fact about these rights today is their pristine integrity and the success with which they can still be invoked against huge odds, whether by Judith Coplon against the public safety (searches and seizures), Jehovah's Witnesses against the flag (freedom of religion), or Henry Ford against the NLRB (free speech).

The property right is in a somewhat different case. It was as sacred as life and liberty in eighteenth-century

49

theory, a man's property, according to Locke, being but an extension of his person. But the formation of a government to secure it to everybody necessarily subjected this right to the legislative power, while protecting it by due process and compensation. Many of the founders also felt, though they did not enact their feeling, that a more or less even distribution of property was the best guarantee that the right to it would remain secure. Richard Price found a good omen in the fact that in Connecticut "the rich and the poor, the haughty grandee and the creeping sycophant [were] equally unknown." Jefferson and Madison counted on the vast public domain, continuously distributed (as in Lincoln's homestead acts), as an important safeguard against a "gross inequality of condition," whose political results they feared. A "gopher democracy" was in those days not so wild a dream. In fact, not wild enough.

That dream degenerated during the nineteenth century exactly in proportion as the philosophy behind it, namely, the belief in equal rights as a law of nature, was supplanted by a wholly different view of the laws of nature. A couple of Englishmen, Darwin and Ricardo, were as responsible as anybody for the change. Vulgarized versions of the survival of the fittest and the iron law of wages turned nature into a jungle and society into a Hobbesian "war of all against all," the solace for these maleficent "facts of life" being supplied by the doctrine of progress. In England there grew up what Matthew Arnold termed a "religion of inequality." All such views, usually summarized as "social Darwinism," reached their American peak during the period of judicial oligarchy, so

that law and the prevailing view of justice alike approved the development of those very "gross inequalities
of condition" that the founders had feared. There was,
of course, enough practical truth in the new doctrines to
make them enormously successful in putting liberty to
the task of creating wealth. The country did "go on . . .
prospering beyond example"—though perhaps not suffi-
ciently puzzled.

By the time of the New Freedom and the New Deal,
when pragmatic reformers with an egalitarian bent set
about correcting some of the excesses of social Darwinism, the true nature of the property right was hopelessly
obscured by the spread of the technological revolution.
A "gopher democracy" (though not without its nostalgic
or Brandeisian adherents) seemed self-evidently incom-
patible with industrial modes of production. The nature
of industrialism has accordingly impeded, as the dust
raised by the New Deal has obscured, the task of this
generation of Americans to restate and reapply their beliefs about the relation of property to life, liberty, and
the pursuit of happiness.

So far, in the attempt to reverse nineteenth-century
inequalities, we have manufactured a darkling atmosphere of chronic social crisis without updating the property right at all. This atmosphere has driven a host of
new powers and responsibilities into the corral of the
federal government in such helter-skelter fashion that
sane men can despair of liberty and of the whole American experiment. The very reasons the founders gave for
fearing a strong central government seem all to have
come true: standing armies, heavy taxes, mountainous

debts, "swarms of officials," a steady narrowing of the "self-determining power" of that "intellectual agent," the free citizen. Has the virgin at last been deflowered? Are we repeating the pattern of democracy-into-despotism, which John Adams called "the history of mankind, past, present and to come"? Democratic absolutism, the danger second only to anarchy in our system, has been pronounced triumphant before. "The evils we experience flow from the excess of democracy," said Elbridge Gerry —in 1787. "The Constitution is a dead letter . . ." a victim of "pure democracy," said Orestes Brownson—in 1844. "What was once a constitutional federal republic is now converted in reality into one as absolute as that of the Autocrat Russia," said Calhoun—in 1850. Those who take the pessimistic view of the nature of man have never lacked occasion for pessimism.

A healthy dose of that same pessimism, however, was written into the Constitution itself and is as responsible as anything for the fact that the U.S. has managed to keep the same form of government longer than any other extant nation. The Constitution is an illustration of the method by which our system combines liberty and equality. It is a method that makes the angriest majority think twice and the subtlest would-be tyrant despair.

The Constitution itself was of course a committee compromise, and was perhaps not seen whole even by many of its authors until some of them began to propagandize it in *The Federalist*. But the principle of limitation, which is the legal essence of constitutionalism, was firmly embedded in its letter and spirit, so much so that it has frequently required very strong Presidents to make it work. The Constitution also provided ample invitation for such Presidents. It is a combination of reed and oak.

Could a majority of U.S. voters, by perfectly legal means, combine to plunder the country and enslave the rest, as Hitler enslaved the Weimar Republic by legal means? In theory, yes. It would require constitutional amendments by a process made intentionally difficult, designed to serve only what Charles Beard called "the matured will of an undoubted and persistent majority." But that matured will has overridden objectors (some of them very violent objectors) eleven times since 1789, and doubtless will again. Except for one provision about the Senate, the amendment process imposes no absolute limits on popular sovereignty. Which helps explain why even the most radical groups in our history (the Abolitionists and Communists being the only important exceptions) have never attacked or renounced the Constitution directly.

But could not a shrewdly led majority subvert the Constitution with or without changing it, as Huey Long subverted the Louisiana constitution? Perhaps. It would encounter two formidable obstacles. It would first encounter the built-in checks and balances, from judicial review to varying tenures, by which power is diffused and poised among the various organs of government, and which forced even the New Deal, in its most active period, to bypass established bureaus and work through its own informal (and highly perishable) machine of dedicated individuals. But even if such a majority could turn the whole government into an instrument of its sin-

53

gle will, it would then encounter the genius of constitutionalism, which resides not merely in our form of
government but in the very nature of our system.

The "consent theory" of government has two major
variations, the mechanical and the organic. Under the
mechanical version, which is pure Locke, consent is
measured by simple enumeration, the will of the nation
being no greater than the sum of its votes; dissent is not
only possible but respectable. But another philosopher
of democracy, Rousseau, had a more ambitious idea. To
him the sum of the votes was something less than, and
might even be different from, a mystic what-is-it called
the General Will, supposed to express the democratic to-
getherness of the citizenry. The body politic, according
to Rousseau, is "a moral being possessed of a will . . .
[and] whoever refuses to obey the General Will shall be
compelled to do so by the whole body. This means nothing less than that he will be forced to be free"—for his
true freedom and in fact his real will, whether he knows
it or not, are inseparable from the General Will, which
"is always right."

This organic theory of democracy, the eighteenth century's inheritance from Plato and bequest to both Napo-
leons and to Hitler, is more exciting than the Lockean
and has had much influence on democratic thought even
in non-totalitarian countries, especially during "crusades
for democracy." It is profoundly different from the American system, whose founders had no use for Rousseau (or
Plato either). Our system is non-organic because it requires no concept of a "state" at all, regards every majority as temporary, and sees the government as a mere

servant, something between an administrative convenience and a necessary evil.

Thus no demagogue could ever successfully arouse
American patriotism by appealing, however discreetly,
to a "General Will" of the American nation. It has always
been possible to argue whether there is such a thing as
the American nation at all in the European sense—apart,
that is, from its obvious dimensions of law, geography,
and population. What holds Americans together, the real
focus of their patriotism and common loyalties, is not a
national organism but the system. And the dimensions of
that system—liberty and equal rights—are as wide as the
world and the human race.

Critics of our mechanical system—for example the English political scientist T. D. Weldon, in his recent *States
and Morals*—correctly point out that it implies an "atomic"
view of society; that its voting integers are bloodless and
arithmetical; that the need for *community*—what the
French mean by *fraternité,* what the English treasure in
feudal relationships, what gives the church in Catholic
lands so indispensable a function—that this deep human
need is nowhere officially recognized or satisfied in the
American system. Our system, the criticism runs, replaced
a society of status by one of contract, but contract is no
substitute for community, and we have left that big
vacuum unfilled. In the absence of "community," we are
told, America is held together only by the "cash nexus."

The criticism is not only largely true, but puts its fin-
ger on the most revolutionary single feature of the American system. America, unless it changes radically, will
never be a community. It is simply the framework for as

55

many communities, and as many different kinds of communities, as the people desire to create for themselves.

The states did not bring thirteen matured examples of free self-government to the Philadelphia convention, to have them distilled into a uniform federal compact. On the contrary, the irresponsibility of many state governments, especially in matters of currency and contract, was one of the reasons for the convention. Hamilton thought the states "ought to be abolished" except as a jurisdictional convenience. There was a compromise between the rights of small states and large, but the issue between "states' rights" and federal power was not so much compromised as evaded in favor of federal power. The issue was raised again later and Calhoun brilliantly inflated it to the doctrine of the "concurrent majority," a wholesale rationale for nullification. But that extreme form of the doctrine would never have been approved by the founders. John Adams had seen it cause the suicide of free Poland ("that noble but ill-constituted republic") in 1767 under the name of *"liberum veto,"* and he would have laughed or wept at the hopes set afloat by the U.N. charter of 1945.

No, "states' rights" are not now and never were the key to American federalism. They are one, but not the chief, of the methods by which federalism limits the federal government's power. Madison came closer to the key in what he called a "multiplicity of interests"; he recognized a diversity of economic classes—debtors and creditors, farmers and artisans, importers and manufacturers —over the face of the nation. The economic base of politics was more obvious to Americans than to Europeans, and what truth there is in the Marxist analysis was not only anticipated by Madison but given a more rational solution. Like John Adams, he believed strongly in the balance of power, within whose interstices freedom can always find a dwelling place. And it finds one even in so closely knit an economy as ours today, in which "classes" have become organized interest groups—labor, business, farm bloc, and the other lobbies—checking and offsetting each other's greed and forcing conscientious Congressmen to work overtime in search of the true area of agreement between them. Which, when found, is a tolerable facsimile of the national sense of justice. Our so-called "secret government" by lobbyists would have seemed no strange or fatal thing to Madison. Said John Adams, "Longitude, and the philosopher's stone, have not been sought with more earnestness by philosophers than a guardian of the laws has been studied by legislators from Plato to Montesquieu; but every project has been found to be no better than committing the lamb to the custody of the wolf, except that one which is called a *balance of power.*"

A multiplicity of interest groups is the negative aspect of constitutionalism, by which any one of them is prevented from monopolizing the government. But constitutionalism also has a positive aspect. It is this: that the *creative* work of self-government, the work that involves the spotting of an inequity or an opportunity, thinking about it, and proposing or performing a reaction to it, is left to the initiative of the people. Constitutionalism, in short, not only protects liberty, but relies on it to be the motor force for the actual organization and improvement of a living society. This positive aspect of constitutionalism is the American solution for two of the oldest problems of political philosophy: the problem of an aristocracy and the problem of the kind and rate of social change.

Adams and Jefferson used to argue about the nature of an aristocracy, but they agreed thoroughly on the need for one. We have one. We call it our "leadership." It is not thought of as an aristocracy because of its rapid turnover, its volunteer quality, and the fact that its motives are not always selfless. It nevertheless serves the purpose of an aristocracy where and when required, whether in a Boy Scout troop, a corporation, a reform movement, or the government (*see* "The Busy, Busy Citizen," Chapter VIII). Private ambition is not demonstrably the worst motive for an aristocracy, and ours is in any case frequently motivated by altruism as well. The other drawbacks of this volunteer system are probably offset by its efficiency: most free men have an instinctive self-knowledge that steers their initiative (when they have any) to the careers and positions they are likeliest to be good at.

The second great problem solved by positive constitutionalism is the rate of social change. The speed of actual social change in America has been obscured in recent years by the greater noise made, or suffering imposed, by sweeping changes decreed or publicized elsewhere, as in Russia, China, and Britain. Because the American system is a fixed system, American society has a reputation for being fixed as well. The reputation is belied by the actual workings of our constitutionalist machine.

As laboratories of change, the states still play a vital role in American life. In the history of American reform they always have "cut paths for each other." Universal manhood suffrage was achieved state by state before it became national policy; Georgia, while still lagging on racial equality, may be pioneering on manhood equality by its recent extension of suffrage to eighteen-year-olds. The difficult unfinished business of the Civil War, equal economic rights for Negroes, is being solved slowly but surely state by state, this method being the best guarantee that when a national FEPC law is passed, it will be a real and enforceable reform, not a paper one. And within the states, every utopian scheme ever blueprinted by European or American dreamers has been tested somewhere on American soil, from Fourier's phalansteries to the single tax—without committing the nation. The biggest single modern experiment, the TVA, though dependent on federal money, could not have been tried if local initiative and state and interstate cooperation had not been available and enlisted to see it through.

Today the area of social experiment deserving the highest priority is the relation of man and his liberty to the machine and the "unnatural" way of earning a living it imposes. The social organ that controls most of the machinery in the U.S., and organizes most of the industrial work, is the corporation. Despite a harassing fire from governments and reformers over its own right to life and liberty, the corporation has become a fairly autonomous

59

and fairly well-dispersed unit in the galactic pattern of our federal system. As such it has important constitutionalist jobs to perform, which it is now undertaking (see Chapter IV, "The Transformation of American Capitalism," and Chapter XI, "Individualism Comes of Age"). The corporation is the place where the man and the machine actually confront each other; it is a laboratory on a human scale; and it is also an actual or potential "community" in the European sense.

Many such industrial communities have achieved a striking degree of happiness and success in America, and the principles of organization that these experiments disclose are likelier to be more widely adopted and adapted under our constitutionalist procedures than under any other. The constitutionalist method can thus still keep America the home of more and better distributed "happiness" than any other—even though the hardy yeomanry of the gopher democracy now carry union cards, and the public domain is subdivided and sewered, and the star-perfumed wilderness has become a forest of presses and drills.

Such is the essence of the American system—liberty, equality, constitutionalism. We have claimed that these principles have timeless and universal application. It remains to explain how and why this is so.

The American federal system, with its strong presidency, independent courts, local autonomies and checks and balances, is not the only conceivable political vehicle for the "Blessings of Liberty," which are its purpose. A parliamentary system like the British, even though theoretically tainted with democratic absolutism, can conceivably continue to avoid that danger, outlast the American divided-powers system, and contribute more than ours to the cause of human liberty in the long run. Nevertheless we believe not only that our system is the best for America, but that the principles of equality and of constitutionalism must be rediscovered and implemented by any people anywhere who take liberty seriously.

Constitutionalism, for example: despite its extremely American accent, what is it but a way of observing the universal truth, best stated by a nineteenth-century English liberal on the subject of India, that "self-government is better than good government"? People should do as much as possible for themselves and by themselves at all levels of society, and there is therefore a presumption against any government, state or national, that proclaims a new need for its own intervention. Said Jefferson, "If we can prevent the government from wasting the labors of the people under the pretense of taking care of them, they must become happy." Says Jimmie Durante: "Don't put no constrictions on da people. Leave 'em ta hell alone." This view sadly needs rediscovering by those many altruistic bureaucrats who, in every nation of the world, are deliberately or absent-mindedly feeding Leviathan in the name of helping or guiding the people.

And equality: what is that but a standing reminder against the cardinal sin of pride? It is a political metaphor for Christian love, the open door that connects class with class, nation with nation, race with race. The Englishman Weldon, who hopes that the U.S. will learn not to try to export democracy, argues that the equal rights of all men are not "self-evident"; that some people, whether in London or in Africa, are "sub-individuals" in fact, whatever they may be in theory. On this view, the unqualified assertion of equal rights is another case of what the English think of as America's worst habit, that of promising more than we can deliver.

They used to throw that one at Lincoln, too. Said he, "They [the authors of 'equal rights'] meant to set up a standard maximum for a free society, which should be familiar to all, and revered by all; constantly looked to, constantly labored for, and even though never perfectly achieved, constantly approximated, and thereby constantly spreading and deepening its influence and augmenting the happiness and value of life to all people of all colors everywhere."

As for liberty—a mere "word"—it remains the heart not only of the American System, but of the American Proposition, that "permanent revolution" in human affairs. We have learned to protect it and extend it within our own democracy. But it is a brittle treasure, for the right to it exists only when that right is believed in, and when its source is believed in. It appears from the American experience that men can govern themselves when they believe in that right. Yet America remains an experiment, however, because Jefferson's most searching question is still unanswered. Wrote he: "Can the liberties of a nation be thought secure when we have removed their only firm basis, a conviction in the minds of the people that their liberties are the gift of God?"

This chapter has little in economic overtones. An extension of the first, it explains that <del>that</del> triad of the American system — liberty, equality, constitutionalism.

PART 2.

American self-government consists in learning how to apply the Proposition to specific American requirements. Here it is shown how this is being done in four important areas: business, politics, labor, and local community affairs.

THE TRANSFORMATION

OF AMERICAN CAPITALISM

WHAT WE HAVE here called the Proposition, together with what we have called the System,
constitute the basis for the permanent revolution that was
brought about in the eighteenth century and for which
the U.S.A. has ever since acted, or tried to act, as the
vehicle. Yet, were this the end of the matter, the revolution would never have come about. For the revolution
was not and is not a mere exercise in political theory. It
was the revolution, as already explained, of the individual human being, and it consequently involved the
transformation of all aspects of human society—not only
the political, but also the cultural and economic. Thus,
having reviewed its major political applications, we can
only understand it if we now turn to an examination of
its applications in these other fields.

With regard to this necessity, however, the authors

have made a somewhat arbitrary decision. We have decided not to enter into a consideration of the applications of the revolution in the important cultural field. Our reasons are, in general, twofold. First, we consider this field, which includes the great questions of religion, the arts, education, learning—all that which pertains to the development of the individual, as such—so important that it requires a whole study of its own if it is to be adequately represented. It could not be covered with any hope of success in one or two chapters. But secondly, while the authors confess to certain ideas in this field, they feel that their unique contribution, both in terms of theory and reporting, lies in that area which is usually referred to as "the economy." This word, we take it, includes something much more than economic theory: it includes business and industry, technology and science, politics and sociology, and so forth. It is an area in which the authors have to a great degree specialized. Moreover, it has been the major domestic battleground of our time. Probably the fundamental problem of freedom is cultural, but for the last quarter-century the struggle for freedom has manifested itself chiefly in questions of political economy all over the world. This area, therefore, we believe, is the strategic one to choose in showing how the permanent revolution is being carried out by Americans in the modern world.

Nothing demonstrates this better than the story of American capitalism itself. Fifty years ago American capitalism seemed to be what Marx predicted it would be and what all the muckrakers said it was—the inhuman offspring of greed and irresponsibility, committed by its master, Wall Street, to a long life of monopoly. It seemed to provide overwhelming proof of the theory that private ownership could honor no obligation except the obligation to pile up profits. It was, indeed, close to the capitalism that Andrei Vishinsky today keeps on denouncing so laboriously and humorlessly. And it was the capitalism that millions of people abroad and many even at home, to the immense aid and comfort of the Communists, still think American capitalism is.

But American capitalism today is actually nothing of the kind. There has occurred a great transformation, of which the world as a whole is as yet unaware, the speed of which has outstripped the perception of the historians, the commentators, the writers of business books—even many businessmen themselves. No important progress whatever can be made in the understanding of America unless the nature of this transformation is grasped and the obsolete intellectual stereotypes discarded.

Many evidences of the transformation are at hand, though they have never yet been drawn together into what is very urgently needed—a restatement of capitalistic theory in modern American terms. Take, for example, the all-pervasive character of American capitalism, as stressed in The American Way of Life. There has been a vast dispersion of ownership and initiative, so that the capitalist system has become intimately bound in with the political system and takes nourishment from its democratic roots. What might be called the influence of Main Street has become vastly more important than the control of Wall Street. U.S. capitalism is *popular* capitalism, not only in the sense that it has popular support, but in the deeper sense that the people as a whole participate in it and use it.

But perhaps the transformation can best be understood by looking at what has happened to "Big Business," which once was supposed to have controlled the economy from its headquarters in Wall Street. The fact is that Wall Street no longer wields much power over Big Business, which in turn is far from being the most powerful sector of the economy. For economic power boils down to the ability to decide who makes what and who gets what and in what proportions, and business alone no longer decides this. "The class struggle in America," writes Professor Clair Wilcox in the *Harvard Business Review,* "is not a struggle between the proletariat and the bourgeoisie. It is a struggle between functional groups possessing concentrated power—a struggle to control the products of industry." These groups, as Professor Wilcox describes them, are Big Labor, Big Agriculture, Big Little Business, and Big Business. Of them all, Big Business, if only because it is subject to the most pressure, exercises its power with a strong and growing sense of responsibility. It has led the way to the formation of a kind of capitalism that neither Karl Marx nor Adam Smith ever dreamed of.

At the bottom of the change is simple morality, which has concerned the U.S. throughout its history, sometimes to the point of fanaticism. "The American," H. L. Mencken once said, "save in moments of conscious and swiftly lamented deviltry, casts up all ponderable values, including the value even of beauty, in terms of right and wrong." Like the European who described moral indignation as suppressed envy, Mencken scorned it as the mark of the peasant; and the American's capacity for moral indignation *has* resulted in many "uncivilized" excesses like prohibition. But it has also made him the most omnivorous reformer in history. Karl Marx based his philosophy on the fatalistic assumption that what he described as the inherent defects of capitalism are above the will of men to affect them. It has remained for the history of U.S. capitalism, beginning as early as the 1870's, to show that the moral convictions of men can change the course of capitalistic development.

And it would have been strange if a nation that had only recently fought a terrible war over the question of slavery had *not* got indignant about the excesses of its "robber barons." People, of course, do not necessarily rise up voluntarily and act on moral indignation. What is essential is their capacity for it; given a free, lively press and plenty of politicians, the action follows. Action followed in the U.S. because a whole school of commentators, from novelists to reporters, from historians to cartoonists, rose up to expose the financial and industrial scandals of the day. There were the Ida Tarbells and Henry Demarest Lloyds, the Upton Sinclairs and Frederick Oppers, backed by the Hearsts, McClures, and Munseys. Some were hypocritical and others wholly sincere, but all operated on the effective principle that the public could be fetched by an earnest appeal to its moral standards.

In their zeal the muckrakers paid little attention to the great economic role played by "robber barons" in forming the capital to lay the rails, erect the factories, build the machinery for a new and expanding economy. Naturally the muckrakers were concerned not with amoral economics but with immoral practices. Their pictures of the American economic brigandage of the late nineteenth and early twentieth centuries became stereotypes all over the world—Daniel Drew feeding his cattle salt to make them drink heavily the day before market; Cornelius Vanderbilt bragging how "we busted the hull damn legislature"; foxy Jay Gould, whom Vanderbilt called the smartest man in America, cornering the national gold-coin supply through his White House connections, and systematically and openly robbing the Erie; gelid old John D. Rockefeller perfecting the trust system and eliminating competitors like clay pigeons. Here was the principle of property ownership carried to its absurd conclusion, capitalism gone berserk. But here also was the moral indignation of the American people. Fanned by lurid accounts in the press and by politicians and publicists of almost every persuasion, from Populists to Republicans, it started the transformation of American capitalism.

Popular resentment of the railroad rate-making came early, even before the muckraking school was in full swing. The Interstate Commerce Act was passed in 1887. And only three years later there occurred what is probably the most portentous single legislative act in the history of American capitalism: the passage of the Sherman Act against monopolies and combinations "in restraint of trade." Although endorsed by all parties, its birth was inauspicious, and the bill was amended almost to death. Senator John Sherman himself, the story goes, never read the final version. And for several years, under Cleveland and McKinley, the act was used little, and then ineffectively. In 1901 J. P. Morgan disregarded it and put U.S. Steel together. "What looks like a stone wall to a layman," said Mr. Dooley, "is a triumphal arch to a corporation lawyer." But the muckrakers began to make themselves felt. In 1902 Teddy Roosevelt, a man who not only understood the public mind but judged almost everything in terms of righteousness, whipped out the Sherman Act and used it as a "big stick" on what he was the first to call the "malefactors of great wealth." He wielded it so effectively against the Northern Securities Co. that the legislation became a power in American life.

The defects of the Sherman Act were soon and widely recognized. "No law can make a man compete with himself," observed J. P. Morgan characteristically. Others noted the great paradox of the antitrust conception: a strong company that really obeyed the law and competed strenuously would end up as a monopoly, violating the law. Contemplating such contradictions, the "realistic" Europeans abstained from trust-busting; they left it to the naive Americans, who in their preoccupation with right and wrong were foolish enough to take so seriously and apply so dogmatically their notions of fairness and justice.

The antitrust law nevertheless acquired stature and authority. However patent its imperfections, however hollow its victories, however vitiated by later acts like Miller-Tydings and Robinson-Patman, it became, in the words of Justice Holmes, "a brooding omnipresence in the sky." Even when businessmen are puzzled and irritated by the letter of the law, they respect its spirit. Even when their lawyers tell them how to get around it, they know they *are* getting around it. The law, in the last analysis, amounts to nothing less than the successful extension of the Anglo-Saxon common law, the basis of the whole English-speaking world's unique liberty, into the realm of business. And its success is among the chief reasons why American business is today so vastly different from European business.

Other reforms came sporadically. The American's moral indignation, naturally enough, did not burn with a steady flame. In good times he tended to overlook violations of his basic notions; in bad times he looked for something to blame things on, and demanded that something be done about them. During the 1920's popular demand for reform was almost nonexistent. For one thing, the scorn of some of the nation's most effective writers made preoccupation with moral issues unfashionable if not ludicrous. For another, business seemed to be doing fine, and seemed to deserve not reform but praise. As the immensely popular *Saturday Evening Post* demonstrated in almost every issue, as Herbert Hoover himself phrased it, "The slogan of progress is changing from the full dinner pail to the full garage."

The catastrophe of depression blasted this dream. The shocked and angry people, seeing their livelihood disappear, put the Right to Life above the other rights. Their natural tendency to blame the bust on those who only yesterday were taking credit for having started an eternal boom was strengthened by revelations such as those of the Pecora congressional investigation into Wall Street financial practices. So they embraced the latter-day Populism of the New Deal, and demanded that something be done. Writers and intellectuals took up the cudgels. Some were merely inclined to condemn what they had for so long contemned, but many tried to find out how and why it had happened, and how to keep it from happening again.

Many of the ensuing reforms survived. Immediately after the Pecora investigation, Congress passed a law divorcing investment banking from deposit banking. And a year later it passed the well-intentioned Securities Exchange Act, which put the Stock Exchange under federal regulation, gave the Federal Reserve Board authority to limit speculative margins, required all officers and stockholders of big companies to report their dealings in their companies' securities, and created the Securities and Exchange Commission to watch over the investment market.

Other attempts at reform were less successful. NRA, for example, went to a well-deserved death. As for the famed Temporary National Economic Committee, much of what it investigated was beside the point by the time it was in print—and not only because of the impending war. Even while the committee was mulling over the power of big business, and the intellectuals were in full cry on the trail of finance capitalism, business initiative had been dispersed among hundreds of enterprises; business power in the aggregate found itself confronted by the rising power of the unions on the one hand, the farmers on the other; and Wall Street had ceased to be a valid symbol of great tyranny.

The decline of Wall Street actually began long before the reforms of the New Deal. It began when corporations grew rich and independent. The rights to their profits, of course, were by traditional economics vested in the stockholders. But their managers saw no point in paying, say, $20 a share in dividends on their stock, when $10 was enough to sustain the company's credit rating. They also reasoned that it was *they,* and not the stockholders, who were directly responsible for the profits. So they began to hold back on the stockholders and put the money into corporate reserves. As early as 1905 the Santa Fe, under Edward Ripley, adopted the policy of a dollar for the stockholder, a dollar for the property. Owen Young of G.E. and others, some years later, further developed the idea of self-capitalization, arguing that the money plowed back would in the long run enhance the stockholder's equity. Whether it did or not, it enabled a large part of business to do its own banking.

Wall Street did not feel the change at first. In the boom of the 1920's the issue of new securities passed the $500-million-a-year mark, and a rich time was had by all. But even then the bulk of the Street's effort was going into the buying and selling of old issues (and new issues of holding companies that used the money to buy old issues), the promotion of dubious foreign bonds, and the lending of money at, say, 7 per cent for the speculative purchase of stock paying, say, 5 per cent. And even then

74

corporations were putting up to ten times as much money into their reserves as all companies were raising in new stocks and bonds. And the depression hit the Street's new-issue function even harder than it hit the trading function. High income taxes and the growing corporate practice of financing new issues through insurance and trust companies trimmed the new-issue business almost to the vanishing point.

Except as its opinions still influence investment policies, Wall Street today exerts only a fraction of the power it once wielded. Industry now plows back 60 per cent of its profits, as against 30 per cent in the 1920's, and the bulk of money used in capital formation comes from corporate earnings or from internal sources such as depreciation. The largest brokerage house on the Street, accounting for 10 per cent of the stock trading on the Stock Exchange, is Merrill Lynch, Pierce, Fenner & Beane, 90 per cent of whose customers are small-fry out-of-towners.

The House of Morgan is still one of the large commercial banks of the country (its underwriting business was passed over to Morgan Stanley in 1935), with total resources of about $667 million; and the phrase "Morgan Company" still evokes images of the old days when Morgan did direct U.S. business. But the working capital of General Motors, by contrast, is more than $1.6 *billion*, and G.M. not only finances itself but recently loaned money to Jones & Laughlin. As for leadership and control, Robert Young's defiance of Morgan in buying control of the C. & O. years ago was more a feat of derring-do than genuine audacity. And when the "Morgan" directors of Montgomery Ward found themselves disapproving Sewell Avery not long ago, they shortly afterward found themselves resigning. The power and the glory had vanished. The dynamic leadership of the economy had moved to the big corporate offices in midtown New York, Schenectady, Chicago, Pittsburgh, and points west and south. It is indeed hard to believe that only thirty-nine years ago J. P. Morgan, the one-man center of the American business universe, was candidly laying his cards on the table at the Pujo investigation: "I like a little competition, but I like combination better. . . . Without control you cannot do a thing."

The cataclysm of the depression, which forever broke apart the old business universe, also heaved up the bright new stars of the unions and the farmers. With between 14 and 16 million members in labor unions, labor leaders now enjoy tremendous industrial power. This power is exercised through the familiar method of tying up an entire industry in order to win certain gains for the workers, whether these gains be "economic" or not. In the face of such power, industry is impotent; and since the national welfare is often enough at stake, the White House itself becomes directly involved. The danger of such power is obvious, and was recently accented by John L. Lewis, who put his miners on a three-day week, not merely to enforce a wage demand, but to keep the price of coal up by creating a scarcity. Here, indeed, is a problem that the permanent revolution has not yet solved, although certain solutions are beginning to emerge, as described in the next chapter. The point to note here is that the power of Wall Street, which has declined in any case, has been met, and sometimes over-matched, by the power of modern labor; a development that has played an enormous role in the transformation of American capitalism.

The power of the farmer, if less direct than that of labor, is likewise formidable. Represented in Congress out of proportion to his numbers, the farmer has been championed by legislators and bureaucrats who have effectively insulated him from the law of supply and demand. By restricting output, fixing prices, and storing up surpluses at government expense, they have done for agriculture what a watertight cartel would do for a group of manufacturers of widely varying efficiency. They have not only saddled the public with high prices, they have, of course, tended to prevent American farming from becoming as efficient as it ought to be and can be. For they have spread a price umbrella over the farmers that has enabled the worst of them to do all right and the best of them to make fantastic and undeserved profits without necessarily encouraging any of them to become more efficient. The $23-billion farm industry, furthermore, is hardly comparable to any one industry; it is more comparable to all industry—to all industry cartelized, subsidized, and rigidified. In terms of deciding who makes what and who gets what, it is one of the most powerful blocs in American history.

And where, in this regrouping of U.S. economic power, do we find the sense of responsibility that ought to go with the power if the nation is to increase its productivity? Labor, with a few exceptions, does not yet show much of it, and agriculture shows even less. The only place it can be found in any force is in the individual business enterprise, which now has the initiative that might have remained in Wall Street had not the transformation taken place.

One of the two chief characteristics of big modern enterprise is that it is run by hired management. As Berle and Means put it, the power inherent in the control of the "active property"—the plant, organization and good will—has superseded the power inherent in "passive property"—the stocks and bonds. Even companies whose owners are managers may be described as management-run. The Ford company, for example, behaves not as an organization solely dedicated to earning the maximum number of dollars for the Ford family, but as an organization dedicated first of all to its own perpetuation and growth.

The other chief characteristic of the big modern enterprise is that management is becoming a profession. This means, to begin with, that a professional manager holds his job primarily because he is good at it. Often he has begun at the bottom and worked his way up by sheer merit. Or more often he has been carefully and even scientifically chosen from a number of bright and appropriately educated young men, put through an executive-training course, and gradually insinuated into the activities for which he shows the most talent. Since even at the top he generally functions as a member of a committee rather than as a final authority, his talents are so well balanced that none of them protrude excessively. He lives on what he makes, and even when he is well paid he doesn't have much left after taxes. Generally he is gregarious, and usually he is not a colossal "personality." But if he is not a General MacArthur, neither is he a Mr. Milquetoast. And if he is expected not to give arbitrary orders, he is also expected not to take them. In most well-run big enterprises, an executive is by definition a man who would object officially to a policy decision he disapproved.

More important, the manager is becoming a professional in the sense that like all professional men he has a responsibility to society as a whole. This is not to say that he no longer needs good, old-fashioned business sense. He does, and more than ever. The manager is responsible primarily to his company as a profit-earning mechanism, and current talk about the corporation as a nonprofit institution is more than a little naive. Any self-respecting businessman would rightly suspect a colleague who allowed he was in business not to make money. The modern enterpriser *should* be in business to make money. His ability to make money is the prime measure of his company's efficiency. If it cannot prosper in the service it supplies to society, or if it cannot persuade society to pay it enough to prosper, it does not deserve to stay in business. Moreover, the good, efficient manager *likes* to make money, and it is mainly because he likes to make money that he does a first-rate job. As the Russians have discovered, when the profit motive does not exist it has to be invented.

But the great happy paradox of the profit motive in the American system is that management, precisely because it is in business to make money years on end, cannot concentrate exclusively on making money here and now. To keep on making money years on end, it must, in the words of Frank Abrams, Chairman of the Standard Oil Co. of New Jersey, "conduct the affairs of the enterprise in such a way as to maintain an *equitable and working balance* among the claims of the various directly interested groups—stockholders, employees, customers, and the public at large." Not all pundits have understood this vital point. In his romantic *Managerial Revolution,* for example, James Burnham described the trend accurately enough but conveyed the idea that somehow the corporate manager is destined to become the Western equivalent of a King Farouk or perhaps an unusually favored commissar. The corporate manager neither is, nor is becoming, anything of the kind. He is part of a group that enjoys power only so long as it does not abuse it—in other words, precisely so long as it does not exercise power the way men and groups of men used to before the capitalistic transformation.

Thus it is not too difficult to define management's responsibility to the stockholder. Management is no longer occupied exclusively with the interests of the stockholder, who often has become a kind of contingent bondholder rather than a part owner, and who rarely exerts any direct influence on the affairs of the company. But management cannot flagrantly disregard stockholders' interests, at least not for long. As the management of Bethlehem and U.S. Steel know well, stockholders can be a considerable nuisance. Even when widely dispersed, they can be induced to take a point of view by proxy. And on the whole, management is treating the stockholders well—despite "abuses" like the habit of holding annual meetings in some out-of-the-way railway station or in Wilmington, Delaware. Almost any good manager can honestly argue that the growing importance of the hired management and its policy of self-capitalization have been to the benefit of the stockholder. Above all, he can argue that the stockholder's long-term interests lie in letting competent, responsible management build up the company and deal justly with employees, customers, and the public.

But modern management exhibits also a sense of responsibility toward its employees, not only to prevent or anticipate the demands of labor unions (though this motive has often been strong) but for the simple, obvious, and honest reason that a satisfied, loyal group of employees is at least as much of an asset as a modern plant or a vital piece of machinery. The trend toward more enlightened employment policies has been growing for years, and while there is still a great distance to go, an old-style capitalist would be appalled by the wide variety of benefits that modern corporations offer those who work for them. There is a growing tendency on the part of blue-chip management to regard a job in the company as a kind of employment package, complete with pensions, savings plan, and numerous "fringe" benefits such as severance pay, maternity leave, hospitalization and medical insurance. Other managements specialize in certain types of benefits. Some, for instance, go in for stabilization of employment. ATF, Inc., as an example, which recently bought into the furniture business, has succeeded in almost eliminating the highly seasonal character of that work. Some companies (Procter & Gamble, Nunn-Bush, Hormel) carry employment stabilization to the point of guaranteeing an annual wage. Others have developed forecasting techniques to anticipate trends and to stabilize employment by leveling out production. Almost every important company now has a pension plan or is in the process of getting one. Many, like Sears, Roebuck, combine pensions with savings plans, so that when an employee retires he takes with him a sizeable capital sum. Others, backed by the Council of Profit-Sharing Industries (276 members), give the workers a cut of profits, with annual bonuses running up to 100 per cent of base wages.

But material benefits, as Elton Mayo and others have demonstrated, are often not as important as job satisfaction—the feeling of having done a good job, and of having it recognized by people who know what a good job is. Related and equally important is the question of real participation in the company's affairs. The problem involved here is tremendous, and it cannot be solved merely by the resolution to do something about it. In one of the Standard Oil affiliates, for example, management was stumped by a case of group dissatisfaction until the president of the company began to talk to the men informally about some of the problems that were plaguing him and his board. "The men showed an immediate and extraordinary interest, and that gradually revealed the source of their dissatisfaction," recalls Frank Abrams. "They had been 'left out of things.'" The point to be noted here is that not every president could have done that. This president obviously had the "something" it takes to put a man across with his employees. And the gradual cultivation of that something is one of the unfinished tasks ahead of management.

This fundamental point is met, and is combined with material incentives, by the "participation" school, which is growing, and whose most promising development is that fostered by Joseph Scanlon of M.I.T. The Scanlon approach actually brings the worker into the enterprise system by giving him a share in productivity decisions and a cut in productivity profits. Since January, 1950, at least a dozen firms, including Stromberg-Carlson of Rochester, New York, have adopted the Scanlon system, and many more are preparing for it. This approach can hardly fail to revolutionize American industrial relations and thus carry further the great transformation in which American capitalism is engaged.

How well American management has actually done by its employees is a question that leads to inevitable debate. The fact is incontestable, however, that it has done better than management anywhere else—and, for that matter, better than management ever dreamed it could, under the old form of capitalism. The problem, indeed, may be to prevent management from becoming overgenerous. For when a company distributes employee benefits that are not compensated by rising productivity, it must in the long run pass the cost increase on to the consumer. Obviously a company *can* be tempted to win employee cooperation easily; a few producers and a single union can combine to gang up on the public.

Thus far, however, it is the modern manager's sense of responsibility to his customer and the general public that gives him his best claim to being progressive. More goods at lower cost (and prices) is the basic principle of American industry, and even companies regarded as anything but socially-minded have built themselves upon it. Many a chemical, for example, has been sold at a progressively lower price without the spur of competition, simply to encourage the market. And most modern managers do worry a good deal about the related subjects of prices, monopoly, and competition. Competition has come a long way since the time of Lord Dewar, who cracked that "competition is the life of trade, and competition is the death of profits." The alternatives today are not monopoly or all-out competition. The Darwinian concept of all-out competition has given way to the concept of a pragmatic or "workable" competition, which, far from being the death of profits, provides, as smart companies know, the soundest way to ensure their survival.

Aside from its value as a foil to antitrust, which can be exaggerated, healthy, workable competition provides a good check on how a company is doing. Take du Pont, which, though almost unique, may well set a precedent. Pursued by the hounds of antitrust (unjustly, it maintains), du Pont spent more than a year looking for a competitor willing to put $20 million into a cellophane plant. Having found one in Olin industries, it is building the plant for Olin and supplying the necessary technical assistance. And that is not all. Because du Pont was the only market source for sodium metal, it induced National

Distillers to make the stuff. And recently it turned over its nylon patents to the Chemstrand Co.

Other companies have learned that a similar self-discipline is the best price policy in the long run. The recent furor about rolling back the prices of automobiles obscures the fact that the automobile companies had conducted themselves with a notable respect for public opinion. Had they let the law of supply and demand take its course in the sellers' market of the past four or five years, they could have priced their cars much higher. Their dealers, it is true, sometimes did extract a premium from eager buyers. But it was the manufacturers' list prices that in the main determined the price level, and the auto makers' refusal to charge what the traffic would bear must be reckoned as an extraordinary example of the transformation of the capitalistic mind.

One of the most pressing concerns of almost every large company today is what people are going to think about it. Board meetings often turn into self-examination sessions, with managers defending or explaining their actions as if before accusing judges. At a recent board meeting of a large consumer-goods company, the president rose up and remarked that the foremen had in effect built up a block between management and labor, and that management was mostly at fault. Fully two hours were devoted to soul-searching and discussion. There was also the matter of closing an old mill in a small town. Not only was the specific situation explored thoroughly, but the history of other similar cases was brought up. This problem was solved, after a full hour's discussion, by the decision to move a storage plant into the town and thus absorb nearly all the displaced employees. As one executive remarked, "At least half our time is taken up with discussing the repercussions of what we propose to do. And this is what the boys who write the books call the managerial revolution."

What may set a new high in business' concern with fundamental values and questions is a current project of Corning Glass Works, which is celebrating its centennial in 1951. On the premise that "As long as there are men making and operating machines, there will be a humanistic problem as well as a scientific and technological problem in an industrial society." Corning has joined the American Council of Learned Societies in sponsoring a conference on "Living in Industrial Civilization." The conference was held in May, 1951, at the Corning Glass Center, and attended by academicians and men of affairs from all over the world. They discussed such topics as Work and Human Values; Leisure and Human Values; the Individual's Sense of Community; Confidence in Life.

Nothing perhaps is more indicative of the corporation's awareness of its responsibilities than the growth of public-relations activities. Upwards of 4,000 companies now go in for public-relations "programs." Although many of them are hardly more than publicity campaigns, more and more managers understand tolerably well that good business public relations is good performance publicly appreciated, because adequately communicated. Now the mere comprehension of a moral axiom, as all parents know, does not guarantee its observance. But its constant iteration does make the subject more and more acutely aware of its importance, and thus eventually influences his behavior. As Paul Garrett of G.M. has been saying for years, "Our program is finding out what people like, doing more of it; finding out what people don't like, doing less of it."

All of which should not be interpreted to mean that business is already rolling us down the six-lane, high-speed highway to economic paradise. We have concerned ourselves here with the pace-setters of American management, and do not presume to imply that all managers and all other companies are doing as well. Many still give precedence to the big, quick profit. Many incline to regard the stockholder mainly as a convenient personification of the profit goal, labor as a lamentably sensitive kind of commodity, and the customer as the man who gets rolled. Like many a labor and agricultural leader, these businessmen try to increase their share of the national product regardless of their contribution to that product. What Professor Wilcox calls Big (or organized) Little Business, for example, is responsible for or protected by most of the fair-trade laws, licensing systems, local bidding laws, and other legal devices that maintain prices independently of the market.

Big Business, too, has something to answer for. Just how much power it has, for example, to fix prices, and to what extent it uses or abuses that power are right now the subjects of much expert contention. Some economists maintain that "Oligopoly is by all evidence the ruling market form in the modern economy"—*i.e.*, since the nation's corporate assets are concentrated in a relatively few companies, the market is made up of a few sellers, who can administer prices. Other economists, attacking the statistics on which such conclusions are based, maintain that only 20 per cent of the national income is provided by unregulated oligopoly, and that an analysis of competition in terms of market realities, which nobody has yet completed, will show that the American economy is becoming more, not less, competitive. It is to be hoped that such an important analysis will be undertaken soon. But whatever its results, it is not likely to reveal that business, socially speaking, has yet attained perfection.

What counts, however, is that certain business leaders *are* setting the pace, and *are* being followed. What counts is that the old concept that the owner has a right to use his property just the way he pleases has evolved into the belief that ownership carries social obligations, and that a manager is a trustee not only for the owner but for society as a whole. Such is the Transformation of American Capitalism. In all the world there is no more hopeful economic phenomenon.

Suitable for use with chapter on capitalism or comparative systems. Could also be used in connection with entrepreneur and corporation

THE U.S. LABOR
MOVEMENT

THE TRANSFORMATION of American capitalism has
been due in large part, as just pointed out, to
the rising power of labor, which has forced a revision of
capitalist thinking and capitalist practices. Yet the fact
that this change has been no more than a *transformation*,
the fact that capitalism in America has not been over-
thrown or seriously damaged by the power of the
workers, is of equal importance to a real understanding
of America. And this fact, which can scarcely be dupli-
cated anywhere in the world, can be accounted for only
by reference to the U.S. labor movement itself.

What utterly baffles the European intellectual concerning the American labor movement is its stubborn refusal to behave in accordance with the so-called "laws of
history." American labor has exhibited none of the ideological uniformity that characterizes continental or

British labor. A vast philosophical distance separates arch-Republican Bill Hutcheson of the carpenters from ex-Socialist Dave Dubinsky of the ladies' garment workers; yet they work together as vice presidents of the American Federation of Labor. And while the younger Congress of Industrial Organizations shows greater cohesion, the differences between Emil Rieve of the textile workers and Walter Reuther of the automobile workers might be enough to disrupt most European trade-union organizations. This diversity runs all the way to the individual local. Within the same union, within the same industry, within the same city, union practices, union policies, and even union oratory vary all over the lot.

American labor is not "working-class conscious"; it is not "proletarian" and does not believe in class war. Some parts of it are as uncompromisingly wedded to rugged individualism as the National Association of Manufacturers. Others want to "reform capitalism." If there were a standard or typical labor view on this subject, it would probably come close to that of George W. Brooks of the strong and tough pulp, sulfite, and paper-mill workers (A.F. of L.), who says "labor's objective of 'making today better than yesterday' is predicated on its acceptance of capitalism."

Yet the American union is a militant union—more militant, perhaps, than its European counterparts. Not only can the average union point to steadier gains for its members in the form of wages and benefits than any counterpart of it elsewhere; it has also been demanding for itself more and more managerial power within the business enterprise. And it is capable of fighting for both its economic and its power demands with a ferocity and bitterness (to say nothing of a vocabulary) that could hardly be matched by any class-war union.

For however much similarity there may be between the objective conditions that gave rise to unionism throughout the industrialized world, the American union is unique in the meaning it has for its member, in the purpose and function it serves for him: *it is his tool for gaining and keeping as an individual the status and security of a full citizen in capitalist society.* That the union has made the worker to an amazing degree a middle-class member of a middle-class society—in the plant, in the local community, in the economy—is the real measure of its success. The existence at the same time of real hostility to enterprise, management, and the economic system among the American workers is not only the measure of its failure; it is the greatest danger to the American labor movement—and perhaps also its greatest opportunity.

Twenty years ago it was easy to dismiss the peculiar characteristics of the American labor movement as signs of the "immaturity" of the American worker. The U.S. at that time, next to Japan, was the least unionized of the major industrial countries. Surely, so the argument ran, a bigger union movement in America would be as proletarian and as much dedicated to class war, as much anti-capitalist and socialist, as the union movements of Europe. The most confident expression of this view came from Harold Laski, the lord high keeper of leftist illusions. But the same view had been held inside the American labor movement itself all during the twenties—for instance, by the young men around the Brookwood Labor College, many of whom later on showed up among the moving spirits of the C.I.O.

Today the U.S. may well be the most unionized of the free countries. Practically all production employees in "big" and "middle" industry are organized. Union contracts determine wage rates everywhere in the land, in unorganized as well as in organized businesses, for clerical as well as for production employees. This switch from an open-shop to an organized economy took only twelve years—from 1933 to 1945. They were years of depression and war, of tension and upheaval. Yet today's successful, strong, and militant labor movement is as little "proletarian" or "socialist" as the small and unsuccessful labor movement of twenty years ago.

Since 1941 there have been three major developments within American labor, all illustrating the same drift: the renascence of the A.F. of L.; the strong anti-ideological shift within the C.I.O.; and the eclipse of left-wing ideologies and philosophies within the labor movement itself.

All through the thirties and right up to World War II the A.F. of L. was the "sick man" of American labor, if not given up for dead. It was obsolete, if not senile; hidebound, unprincipled, inflexible, corrupt, and—worst swear-word of all—"petty bourgeois." Yet today the A.F. of L. has some eight and a half million members—twice as many as it had in 1941. In addition, the bulk of the "independent" unions are A.F. of L. unions in their philosophy, their tactics, and their structure, though not in formal affiliation. Almost two out of every three American union members—10 million out of a total of 15 million—are thus organized on the A.F. of L. basis and in unions that derive in unbroken descent from Samuel Gompers.

Neither economic developments nor the small changes in tactics that have occurred within the A.F. of L. fully explain this renascence. Perhaps it is too much to claim, as some A.F. of L. men do, that it is precisely its anti-proletarian, pro-capitalist character that has been attracting the American worker. But one thing at least is sure: that the A.F. of L.'s middle-class character has proved no obstacle to its success, let alone, as was so confidently predicted only ten years ago, fatal to its very survival.

The C.I.O. at its start was hailed as the fulfillment of the intellectual's dream of a "class-conscious" and "proletarian" labor movement. What has actually been happening to the C.I.O. may be read in the career of the one bright young C.I.O. radical of fifteen years ago who actually made good, the automobile workers' Walter Reuther, by all odds the most dynamic personality in American labor today.

Where Walter Reuther stood politically was never exactly clear. He was certainly not just an "ordinary socialist." There was always a strong resemblance to the Henry Ford of thirty years ago—the Henry Ford who sent the "Peace Ship" to Europe to stop World War I, who had an opinion on anything and everything, and whom the Chicago *Tribune* once called an "anarchist."

There was also a bit of the technocrat in Walter Reuther, this being the element of continuity in his many "Reuther Plans." But there was no doubt whatever that he also believed in the class struggle, in some form of socialism, and in a labor party to bring about the "necessary change in the system." These beliefs (rather than his ability and competence as a union leader) gained him the admiration of all the sentimental "friends of labor" among the intellectuals, from the *New Republic* to the amateur politicians of Americans for Democratic Action.

Yet the biggest labor event of 1950—if not of the entire post-World War II period—was a contract negotiated by Walter Reuther that goes further in its affirmation both of the free-enterprise system and of the worker's stake in it than any other major labor contract ever signed in this country. The General Motors contract is the first that unmistakably accepts the existing distribution of income between wages and profits as "normal," if not as "fair." This at least was the interpretation that was given within the U.A.W. itself to the acceptance of the existing wage structure as the basis for the next five years. It is the first major union contract that explicitly accepts objective economic facts—cost of living and productivity—as determining wages, thus throwing overboard all theories of wages as determined by political power, and of profit as "surplus value." Finally, it is one of the very few union contracts that expressly recognize both the importance of the management function and the fact that management operates directly in the interest of labor.

The G.M. contract probably reflects what Reuther himself has come to believe over the last few years—

though he will surely continue to talk his old line and to ride it hard in his two union publications, the *United Automobile Workers* and *Ammunition* (two of the liveliest pieces of aggressive journalism in the country today). But his own beliefs or words are really none too relevant. The important thing is that this contract—whose significance everyone in the labor movement grasped immediately—has become the program on which Reuther hopes to unify American labor under his own leadership. This is strong evidence of the C.I.O.'s shift toward the George Brooks concept of unionism, "predicated on its acceptance of capitalism." And the force behind the shift is precisely the C.I.O.'s success in gaining for the unskilled and semiskilled worker in the mass-production industries what has been the goal of American labor in general: middle-class status and full citizenship.

Never have left-wing ideologies had so little influence on the American labor movement as they have today. The Communists still control a small but strategic sector of American labor and have scattered but dangerous beachheads elsewhere, notably in the Ford local of the automobile workers. But in glaring contrast to twenty or even to ten years ago, the Communists stay in control only by claiming to be "bona fide unionists"; the mask is dropped only in the closed conventicles of the faithful. David Dubinsky pointed out in 1950 that the old radical, socialist, and idealist movements which formerly were the source of union leaders have been drying up. There are no Wobblies today, no Jewish Bund, no Italian anarchists, no Debs, no Mother Jones. If there is any ideological influence in American labor today it is Catholic union theory—spread by a growing number of labor priests and Catholic labor schools. It is of considerable importance in several C.I.O. unions as well as in the building trades of the A.F. of L.

In historical perspective it appears that the flare-up of left-wing ideologies in the middle thirties was a freak, no more typical of the basic trends of American unionism since the 1890's than the economic stagnation of the period was typical of the basic trends of the American economy. In origins (Knights of Labor, etc.) the American labor movement was more socialist than the British, and in 1902 the A.F. of L. convention barely defeated a resolution endorsing socialism (4,897 to 4,171). This date corresponds to the date when British labor took the opposite turning—1899, when Keir Hardie committed the T.U.C. to the borning Labor party. Since then British labor has been increasingly dominated by the socialist intellectual. By contrast, the creed of the American labor movement, as summed up in that famous sentence of the Clayton Act of 1914, "The labor of a human being is not a commodity or article of commerce," traces back not to the *Communist Manifesto* but to that blackest of "black Republicans," Mark Hanna, whom Gompers joined in the leadership of the National Civic Federation.

This anti-proletarian and non-ideological character of American unionism is the key to its unique achievement, to its greatest danger, and to the method by which it may extend the achievement and avoid the danger. Let

us first consider the achievement, which is the democratic one of integrating unionism with American community life.

Any proletarian union movement, with its class-war
creed, regards the existing community and its institutions as "instruments of oppression." All European union
movements, including the British, have sought to build
their own community organizations in competition with,
if not in opposition to, those of "capitalist society." The
American union movement, by contrast, accepts the community and its institutions.

In 1942 the C.I.O. was represented on ninety commu-
nity-service programs; last year the number was 7,000.
In Akron alone—the bloody labor-management battleground of the thirties—sixteen C.I.O. people serve on various boards of the Community Chest. "We're in about
everything in this town except the Portage Country
Club," said one C.I.O. leader to John Dos Passos. There
is still plenty of resistance by "polite society" against accepting the union leader. But the resistance is hardly
more strenuous today than that always offered to the
newcomer—for example, the resistance of the New York
"society" of merchants and bankers in the 1870's and
1880's to the new industrial magnates.

In some places—one-industry towns with a strong
union like Saginaw, Michigan, and the paper and pulp
towns of Wisconsin—even this resistance is disappearing.
There union men are accepted by the groups that run
the communities and set the mores: the Parent-Teacher
Association and the school board, the elders of the
churches, the hospital board, the volunteer firemen, and

the dramatic society. Even the "service clubs" of the small businessman, such as Rotary or the Lions—once strongholds of anti-union sentiment—are beginning to bring union men in as members. There is also increasing acceptance of union men as normal and regular members in management workshops and panels. For years, of course, union leaders have delivered set speeches to such groups as the American Management Association and the National Industrial Conference Board. But now they are coming more and more into the small, informal, off-the-record groups where the real work is being done— and as men who have something to contribute to a common problem, not just under a flag of truce as emissaries of an enemy power. And there has been full union support for the Joint Council of Economic Education, an amazingly successful group of educators, businessmen, and unionists who are trying to educate Americans in the facts of the free-enterprise system through teaching high-school teachers.

There is a price for these achievements of democratic unionism. The less class war, the more group greed: a quiet division of loot or assumption of privilege at the expense of less organized members of society. Here is the peculiar danger posed by American labor to a free and mobile society: the danger of social thrombosis, of union feudalism.

Last November, Pan American Airways pilots threatened to strike. Their objective was not higher wages, shorter hours, or different working conditions. It was to deny jobs and benefits to a group of fellow pilots. Pan

American had just acquired American Overseas Airlines. But the Pan American pilots refused to let the American Overseas pilots come in except at the very bottom. Union leaders and government agencies both urged full acceptance of the seniority gained by the American Overseas men during their years of service—in vain. The demand of the Pan American pilots was not motivated so much by fear of damage as by desire to gain a better position for themselves—at the expense of fellow pilots who had been unlucky enough to work for the less successful company.

The pressure for *exclusive* kinds of job security usually comes from the men and is often resisted by union leaders. It is in part an instinctive assertion of the property right—a property right in a certain job. The blame, if blame there be, lies not at the door of unionism but in the technical conflict between machine modes of production and American democratic ideals. It seems harder nowadays (though it may not be) to reach the top through individual effort in an industrialized economy. The workers respond to this supposed sacrifice of vertical mobility by claiming more security—and when this claim is asserted in a particular job, the result may be a real loss of horizontal mobility.

Union policy is not responsible for this danger, but the structure of U.S. unionism has paralleled and sharpened it. The value of the union card is highest in a small unit: there is one local per company, if not per plant or even per department. Seniority rights tend to be bounded by the local's membership. So are the "fringe benefits"—

pension rights, severance pay, vacations, sick pay, profit shares, life insurance, etc.—benefits worth as much as 30 cents in some companies for every dollar paid in straight wages. The growing demand for these benefits is in itself a sign of the middle-class character of the American worker and of his union. They are among our major tools of integrating the worker into industrial capitalism as a full and responsible citizen. And they are necessarily grounded in his membership in one particular enterprise or in one particular industry. But these privileges and benefits are usually not transferable. They thus create the danger of tying the worker to his job. After a few years of service a man has amassed too big a stake to be willing to leave, even for a better job. They may also tend to convert the job into a property and the work group into a closed guild. In the typographical union a "priority system" protects a preferred job for a linotype operator even if the worker is forced out for years by illness—or, as in the last war, even leaves the industry for a defense job. Companies with generous pension or profit-sharing plans are under increasing pressure to restrict the hiring of new workers to sons or relatives of their present employees. The fear of just such "un-American" developments was partly responsible for the no-closed-shop provision of the Taft-Hartley Act.

But to halt or reverse this trend will require more than restrictive legislation. It will require considerable imagination in devising new techniques and procedures— above all, techniques to make job benefits transferable. It may also require enabling legislation, the kind that encourages and rewards voluntary action. In attempting to solve this problem we will have to be careful not to weaken the desire of the American worker and of his union for a stake in the enterprise.

We also must not sap the strength of the local unit of unionism. For the vigor and autonomy of the local constitute one of the distinctive traits of American labor, indispensable to its development along democratic rather than proletarian lines. The local has grown strong because American labor, like so many other of our institutions, found it necessary to organize itself on the hallowed American principle of federalism. This followed from the physical nature of the country, from the spirit of its society, and from labor's approach to its task. The English, French, or German union can be satisfied with one national center of power and authority. The American union demands two centers of about equal strength and vigor, the local union and the national union.

A *national*, or industry-wide, organization of real strength is needed to prevent domination of the locals by management. It is needed to set policy, to develop standards for wages and contracts, to represent the union to public and government, and to accept responsibility for the economic and social effects of labor's actions. For every management that feels it would have no labor-relations problems if only it could work exclusively with the "local boys," there is another that has had to ask for the help and intervention of the national officers to settle a local situation that had got out of hand.

National policies and wage rates, however, are no more

101

than the skeleton of American labor-management relations. The local is their flesh and blood. The local develops the spirit of the relationship as well as the rapidly growing "common law," the body of grievance settlements and arbitrator's decisions that define the rights and responsibilities of both parties. As with the federal structure of our system of government, so in the labor movement: local autonomy makes experimentation possible. While bad labor-management relations can be caused by national union officers alone, good union relations require good locals. Even in large companies such as General Motors, in which mutual distrust is profound, and in which as a result all authority is apparently concentrated in the hands of top-management and top-union leadership, patterns of living and working together are quietly but steadily being developed by local union leaders and by the local plant managements with whom they deal day by day.

Federalism is a difficult political system, and many or most American unions have not yet learned how to use it. The national leader is greatly tempted to centralize all power in his own hand, if only to remove threats to his tenure of office. In a few unions, notably John L. Lewis' coal miners, this has led to an all but complete destruction of local life and local autonomy; the locals are not much more than administrative units. Equally great is the temptation for the local leader to declare himself independent; in some of the railroad brotherhoods this has almost fragmented the union into a loose league of warlords whose feuding makes responsible unionism impossible. While unionism was struggling for recognition, these inherent constitutional problems could be brushed aside. Now they are coming to the fore—so much so that more than one union has hired a professional management consultant to strengthen its internal structure.

When that structure is stronger, American labor will have the right machinery for consolidating and extending its traditional goal and for avoiding the danger of feudalism ahead of it. It can fulfill the worker's desire for full citizenship in a non-class society, and keep that society open and mobile. It can—if that is what the worker continues to want.

Many signs point to his still wanting these goals. All kinds of sociological studies reveal his desire to take pride in his job, in his product, and in the company he works for. As his income rises he wants to buy stock in that company through some form of payroll deduction—a desire that has been voiced in companies large and small such as the Bell System, G.M., and Cleveland Graphite Bronze. One of the best popular guides to the reading of corporate balance sheets and corporate profit-and-loss statements was printed two years ago in the A.F. of L. house organ, *Labor's Monthly Survey;* and the Detroit *Labor News* recently ran an admirable treatise on investment and small-estate management. The visiting teams of businessmen and union leaders who have been studying American productivity under ECA auspices were all struck hard by the American worker's acceptance of increased productivity as in his own interest, by his pride in being a worker, but also by his acceptance of the management function as necessary to his own effectiveness.

All this is true—truer than ever. Yet it is not the entire truth. There is also another picture of the American worker—and it is the one major discord in the harmony of the American Proposition. We cannot assert that the big job of industrial society has been done, or that the industrial worker will surely remain "deproletarianized" in the U.S. For there undoubtedly runs a powerful undercurrent of hostility to management and to enterprise, to competitive economy and to profits, throughout the American working class. There are only a handful of conscious collectivists in American labor. But throughout it there is a strong acceptance of anti-enterprise union oratory, a steady support of collectivist and anti-business legislation. And an attitude that sees in enterprise and management THE ENEMY—rather than the opposing team in a rough and competitive game—is a proletarian attitude.

We cannot blame this attitude on the "foreign agitator corrupting the good American workingman" as management was wont to do only a few years ago. It is indigenous, and shared by the skilled "aristocrat of labor" as well as the unskilled man on the assembly line. We cannot explain it away as "economic illiteracy" that will yield to high-powered campaigns of "economic education." But we equally cannot explain it as expressing the "real" desires of the American worker, as the left-wing intellectual is prone to do; the evidence is all the other way. The explanation does not even lie in past management sins. It lies in something much more difficult to change: lack of imagination on the part of managements and union leaders.

The American worker definitely wants to be a part of the business enterprise. He wants to consider it "his" business, its future "his" future, its prosperity "his" prosperity. But his everyday experience is one either of conflict or of lack of relationship between the interests, the prosperity, the profitability of the business and his own interests, his own prosperity, his own future.

The worker is told that his wage, his standard of living, and his job depend on the profitability, stability, and productivity of the enterprise. He knows that. But this relationship is not immediate, not visible, not part of the daily relationship between man and company. It has no impact on the worker's experience. What is real is all too often the opposite: conflict, or the total lack of mutuality of interest.

One illustration must suffice. It is possible to understand why managements were caught so unprepared by the 1949–50 pension wave. But what is totally impossible to understand is why managements did not use the pension demands to make crystal-clear the connection between the company's prosperity and the employee's old-age security. There are proved ways in which this could have been done, simply and dramatically. Yet, as a result of management's handling of the issue, pensions to the worker have become another experience of conflict between his needs and the objectives of business, between "human values" and "greed."

It is the biggest challenge to American management today to design institutions that will tie the needs of business and of the capitalist system (profitability, independent management, investment of risk capital, productiv-

105

ity) directly and visibly to the major interests of the worker (income, job security, recognition and participation, promotional opportunities). Until this is done the American worker will not be able to be what he wants to be, a full citizen in a free-enterprise industrial society. Despite his beliefs he will be pushed by his daily experience into pressing for more and more anti-business laws, more anti-business taxes, and more government welfare. He may even, in an economic or political emergency, develop a susceptibility to that very collectivist infection to which he has hitherto shown such singular resistance. But the development of new and positive policies that will institutionalize the worker's stake in the business enterprise and his responsible citizenship in capitalist society is equally a major challenge to union leadership. The anti-business undertow is a danger to American unionism as well as to business. It tends to push the union leader into opposition to the spirit of American society—a position in which he cannot function. But above all it is only in and through such policies that the American labor movement can develop what it so conspicuously lacks today: the appeal of ideals and of moral leadership. The very strength of the anti-business undertow is proof that it is not enough for a union movement to be free from a class-war and proletarian ideology. It has to have positive beliefs—or it will be in constant danger of infiltration by the very ideologies it rejects.

The left-wing critics of the American labor movement were wrong when they predicted its conversion into a European-type proletarian movement. But they were right in their assertion that it is not enough for labor to define its beliefs and aims in Sam Gompers' famous answer to the question as to what labor wants: "More." Only a positive acceptance of the American Proposition, a positive creed, will strengthen both American society and the American labor movement. Only positive policies will make the union an instrument for the worker's responsible citizenship in capitalist society rather than just a device for getting more from it.

There are labor leaders who realize this and who work devotedly to develop such a policy. There is Clinton Golden—formerly of the steelworkers, now Labor Adviser to ECA—who has directed the research for *Causes of Industrial Peace*. There is Joseph Scanlon—also formerly of the steelworkers, now at M.I.T.—whose exciting work, already referred to in the previous chapter, has been discussed in FORTUNE, January, 1950. There is the work done by the unions in the once strife-torn pulp and paper industry in the Pacific Northwest. But by and large today's union leadership cannot do the job. It has—almost without exception—risen to leadership in the bitter and violent fight for union recognition. Their very background makes it all but impossible for these men to take the lead in integrating the worker and the enterprise into one industrial society. As judicious and as conservative a man as Philip Murray, for instance, cannot help using the usual hate rhetoric of union negotiations, though it both embarrasses and frightens him.

But today's labor leaders are largely at the end of their careers. Even in the young C.I.O., few unions have a young leadership. The majority will retire or die within the next ten years. Mostly their places will be taken by new men, unknown today. These leaders of tomorrow will be men of a very different background: men who have come up in the leadership of a local rather than in organizing a national union, who have learned their unionism after recognition, rather than in the battle for it, and who have served their apprenticeship in day-to-day living and working with management. It is to those men that we will have to look for the resolution of the major conflict within American society.

Looked at one way, American laboɪ has reached maturity. The last decade has proved the validity of its basic concept—the concept that was formulated fifty years ago when the young and small A.F. of L. turned its face against socialism. Looked at another way, the history of American labor is just about to begin. For it is only now that it has achieved power and recognition that it faces its real challenge: to make fruitful its beliefs, its aims, and its power. The potential at least is there.

THE POLITICAL
PARTIES

But if European intellectuals, with their keen sense of logic, are baffled by the American labor movement, which falls far short of what in their view would be logical consistency, they are at a loss when it comes to a comprehension of the American political parties. At least in the labor movement there are certain familiar patterns, and where these are broken the explanations are not too far to seek. But with regard to the political parties, the patterns are less discernible and the deviations more difficult to explain. On the other hand, an understanding of the political parties is quite as important to the meaning of America as an understanding of the labor movement. Indeed, it is probably more so. For the American political parties are rooted in what we have called "constitutionalism," which is, in turn, basic to the entire American system. At the same time, they are the only vehicles through which labor, or any other group, can achieve legitimate political power. They are central, therefore, to the whole theme of America, and were they personified, they might well use the words of Milton's Satan, "Not to know me argues yourselves unknown."

The bafflement of the European intellectuals with regard to American politics, it should be noted, is almost matched by that of Americans themselves. Of course, since party politicking goes on most of the time, most Americans feel that they know all about it; but this is rather more a feeling than a fact. Relatively few Americans really know how the parties work. Their contact with politics is more or less confined to election time, when the whole country is seized by a kind of fever—not infrequently in the midst of a grave international crisis. The land is then filled with oratory. Radio channels become clogged. Newspapers seethe with editorials and paid political ads; the mails are loaded with political literature; loudspeakers on trucks prowl the streets day and night; and millions of buttons proclaiming this or that candidate blossom suddenly from the lapels of otherwise sober jackets. The newest arrival on this hectic scene is television, which is rapidly proving itself the most powerful of all political media. In the 1950 gubernatorial campaign in New York State, Thomas E. Dewey, fighting for his political life, purchased eighteen hours of television, radio, and telephone time during a single day at a cost of $20,000.

Indeed, the cost of all this is prodigious, although, owing to the inadequacy of the election laws, it is always impossible to determine what it really is. The Hatch Act limits the expenditure by any one committee in any one national campaign to three million dollars; however, the limitation is circumvented in various ways. A legitimate way is to multiply the number of campaign committees, which can be done indefinitely; an illegitimate way is to pass around "green money"—that is, unreported cash. In any case the actual totals may greatly exceed the official ones. Thus the Democrat, William O'Dwyer, reported an expenditure of $600,000 for a mayoralty campaign in 1949; but his opponents estimate his actual expenditures at over a million, and their charge has never been denied. The Republicans, as the record shows, can be just as lavish.

The net impression created by such campaigning is that momentous issues are at stake, involving the life and death of the country. Sometimes, of course, that is so; yet American politicking is not necessarily the life-and-death matter it appears to be. It is easily misunderstood, not only by foreigners but by Americans themselves. There is a strong temptation, for example, to liken an American political party to a European political party, to identify the Democratic party with the British Labor party and the Republican party with the British Conservative party, to imagine that these two are slugging it out for the survival of Something as against Something else. Yet the genius of American politics is quite different from that of the politics of Europe, even of Britain. No matter what the orators may say, Americans live in fundamental *agreement* concerning certain long-range aims and principles, outlined in the chapters entitled "The American Proposi-

111

tion" and "The American System." It is fallacious to suppose that political parties under such circumstances will behave in the same way as political parties behave where such fundamental agreement does not exist. Failure to avoid this fallacy, indeed, can lead to serious mistakes in the appraisal of American policies. On the other hand, an understanding of how the parties really do work is essential to an understanding of the permanent revolution.

The American party system was brought about in the first place by the conflict in George Washington's Cabinet between Hamilton, the father of the Federalist party, and Jefferson, the founder of the old Republican party. Ever since then, with minor deviations, the U.S. has had a "two-party" system. The old Republican party became the Democratic party in 1828 and has remained in existence ever since, having been in power for fifty-eight out of one hundred and twenty-two years of its long life. The opposition to the Democratic party has been in power more years (sixty-four altogether) but has shown much less party stability. The Federalist party was replaced by the Whig about 1830 and the Whig by the modern Republican party about 1854. Aside from these major parties, there have of course been many political movements, a few of which, like Theodore Roosevelt's Bull Moose and La Follette's Progressive party, temporarily reached national scale. But American politics has shown an extraordinary bias toward simple bipartisanship. The handy explanation for this, and the one most frequently attempted, is that some profound philosophical or ideological difference separates Americans into two camps.

Modern scholars, such as the younger Arthur Schlesinger, for example, attempt to confirm this distinction historically, and to make it appear that the story of American politics, like that of European politics, is the story of a struggle between "right" and "left," "have" and "have-not," "conservative" and "liberal," for the domination of American affairs.

Yet this interpretation falls short of the realities. It runs into difficulties, for example, in connection with the "platforms" that the parties issue every four years after prodigious soul-searching. These platforms are apt to be almost identical—*vide* the platforms of 1948. Furthermore, relatively few candidates ever stand for the whole of the platform they are supposed to represent. The "party line" is used more as a political convenience than as a matter of conviction. There is, indeed, a kind of unspoken agreement, which the public tolerates most of the time, that a man running for office on a party ticket represents the platform only in a general way and is entitled to differ with his party to the point of outright contradiction on specific issues.

Under such circumstances conventional political categories such as "right" and "left" are almost useless: both are scrambled together as in an omelet. Indeed, in the course of time each party has found itself on both sides of many issues (e.g., states' rights, internationalism, labor, agrarianism, etc.). It is true that the old Federalists and the modern Republicans have to a large extent represented the property-owning class. But the Republican party at its best denies the existence of any such "class," pointing out that the vast majority of Americans are property owners, while the remainder are potentially so; and that everyone in the country, therefore, has a stake in property rights. On the other hand, plenty of "property owners" are Democrats, not only in the South (where every property owner is one) but also in the North, where some of the biggest fortunes are tied in with Democratic politics. The struggle of the "have-nots" against the "haves" has played a strong role in American politics—but not according to any standard party pattern.

Of course, some issues have remained fairly constant. The Republicans have stood consistently for "sound money," whereas the Democrats have a tendency to propound monetary "heresies," such as free silver and deficit spending. Yet even on the battered issue of the tariff the lines break. Republican William McKinley was one of the first to propose a reciprocal-trade policy working toward lower tariffs; William Howard Taft attempted to set up a treaty with Canada to that effect; and many Republicans have backed the reciprocal-trade policy of the Roosevelt and Truman regimes.

It is just as difficult to apply standard political categories to the leaders that the parties have nominated. George Washington himself (who preceded the political parties) belonged to what modern intellectuals would call the conservative tradition; but he led a revolution against his king, and was the prime mover in setting up a new nation under the sun, based upon the most radical principles of the day. Even Hamilton, whom most intellectuals regard as an arch-conservative, did not act like one; at the age of twenty he was a fiery aide to the rebel chief,

114

and as first Secretary of the Treasury he planned the gigantic pioneering task of setting up a system of manufactures in a wilderness. In a recent article in FORTUNE A. Whitney Griswold, President of Yale, pointed out that the agreement between the supposedly conservative John Adams and the supposedly liberal Jefferson was far more profound than their differences. Abraham Lincoln, the first Republican President, did indeed *conserve* the Union; but he also *freed* the slaves—a step more "liberal" than Jefferson himself had been willing to take, despite the urging of his fellow-Virginian, George Mason. Mark Hanna, the intellectuals' symbol of black reaction, was a pioneer, through the National Civic Federation, in developing the rights of American labor. And Theodore Roosevelt, fervid Republican, rattled the nation's teeth with his attacks on the trusts and his espousal of a whole series of progressive policies, domestic and foreign.

By the same token, the Democratic party, supposedly "liberal," has produced some of the nation's greatest conservatives. Such a figure as Calhoun can hardly be fitted into the liberal category. Lincoln's opponent, Stephen Douglas, argued for human slavery. Grover Cleveland, the only Democrat able to win through to the White House during the last third of the nineteenth century, was a pronounced conservative. And today it would be impossible to make a list of powerful Democratic leaders without mentioning Senator Harry Byrd of Virginia, who, while shunning the fanaticism of many of his southern and western Democratic colleagues, is well to the "right" of dozens of Republican leaders.

All this is not to say that there is no distinction between the Republican and Democratic parties. There are a great number of distinctions, but they must be described as "organic" rather than ideological. The nearest approach to a strictly ideological distinction, perhaps, has to do with the question of wealth. The Republican party was founded early in the Industrial Revolution, and one of its chief tasks was to solve the problem of industrial production, concerning which the Whigs had had little to offer. The *production* of wealth, therefore, became a key Republican concept. The Republicans have always worked out their policies from there; such diverse measures as the freeing of the slaves, high wages, the antitrust laws, high tariff, sound money, and overseas expansion at the turn of the century have all been grounded in the idea of production. The Democrats, on the other hand, base their policy making on the idea of the *distribution* of the wealth, whether in terms of land (Andrew Jackson), money (Bryan), or economic security (F. D. Roosevelt). In this sense—the redistribution of the wealth from the top downward—the Democrats can lay claim to a "liberal" tradition. The distinction, however, is limited, because it is chiefly a question of accent. Both parties are for productive expansion and the raising of the standard of living for all.

The truth is that the American political system persists on a bipartisan basis precisely because it is *not* founded on an ideological split. If the parties were primarily doctrinal, then the complex nature of modern society would inevitably bring forth a multiparty system, as it has in Europe. But the genius of American politics lies in the fact that the debates between the parties are concerned, not with first principles, but with how those principles can best be realized in the government of the nation's affairs. The tendency, therefore, is to hold the debate to the pragmatic level—with some oratory thrown in to make it appear otherwise. In short, as contrasted with political parties elsewhere, which are generally based upon doctrinal differences that give rise to partisan conflict, the American parties are like big clubs—more specifically, like athletic clubs, whose aims are both competitive and social. The purposes of these clubs are to win political power and to distribute political patronage. To that end they adopt platforms and define policies, which are then submitted to the voters; but it is important to note that the party precedes the platform.

The first word to learn in American politics, therefore, is "organization." An American party organization is vast and complex, varying in the forty-eight states, and even to some extent in the 3,070 counties. The organization rests ultimately upon 125,000 election districts, the smallest political units; but even these vary in size and method of organizing. Thus in California an election district comprises 200 voters or less; in Illinois from 500 to 800.

All the people in the party with ideas to peddle sooner or later run up against the much-maligned election district leader. This gentleman's primary task, some people forget, is not to win elections: it is, rather, to hold the organization together by (1) getting as many voters as possible to register as members of his party, and (2) "delivering" these voters on primary day for the organization candidate (that is, the man whom the leader supports and who will, in turn, support the leader). What the district leader dreads most is a rebel who challenges the organization leadership, and who, if he wins, will have the power to change it. Sometimes the rebel has a big popular following, and hence a better chance than the organization candidate of winning on election day. When this happens the leader is trapped. Usually his way out of the trap is to knife the rebel, even if this means the defeat of his party at the polls.

In some cases (New York City, for example) the next higher organization officer is the assembly district leader, and above him, in turn, is the county leader. The latter may be a very powerful factor in party affairs. It is true that the county leader is outranked by the state chairman, who in most states is elected by all the county leaders at a state convention, and who may be the direct nominee of the governor, the head of the party in the state. Yet the state chairman cannot fire the county leader, who is elected by his own organization people and who is therefore in a position to take a great deal of initiative if he wants to. The county leader is thus in many ways the kingpin of U.S. organizational politics.

But because of the peculiar structure of the American political system, the matter does not end there. The federal system is superimposed upon the state system, and to some extent intertwines with it. While the parties are organized basically on state lines, it is necessary, for the sake of cohesion, to provide for united action at the national level. This is supposedly done by the national committeemen—one man and one woman from each state and territory, who form the party's national com-

118

mittee. The position of these officers, however, is some-what anomalous. In their home states they enjoy a certain prestige; but the reality of their power is dependent upon victory in the national election, which alone can give them the power to pass out important jobs. In the event of defeat, such jobs go to the committeemen of the other party and there is consequently little to hold the defeated organization together at the national level.

All this is summarized in the position of the chairman of the national committee, who is usually appointed by the party's presidential candidate and acts as the candidate's manager during the campaign. If the candidate wins, the national chairman acquires great power because he speaks for the President, who is of course head of the party. Under these circumstances he can dispense an enormous amount of patronage, and even make his voice heard in matters of policy. But if his candidate loses, the national chairman is in a sorry plight. He has as titular head of his party a defeated man, who cannot dispense any patronage whatever; he himself, therefore, has no jobs to give out. Moreover, rival candidates within the party, who failed to get the nomination, but who hope for it next time, rise up against him; they blame him for the way the campaign was conducted, even though the candidate and his kitchen cabinet, not the chairman, probably made the important decisions.

The Republican party today illustrates what can happen under these circumstances. It resembles nothing so much as a system of Chinese warlords. Its titular head, Governor Thomas E. Dewey of New York, has no real power outside of his own state. Against him there is pitted another Republican party under Senator Robert A. Taft, having its headquarters in Ohio, with a platform quite different from that of the Dewey Republican party. Then there is the Warren Republican party in California, the Duff Republican party in Pennsylvania, the Peterson Republican party in Nebraska, the Driscoll Republican party in New Jersey, and so forth. All these men have been elected in their own right in their own states and do not have to pay any attention to National Chairman Guy Gabrielson, whose job is to bring about party "unity." Mr. Gabrielson's task, virtually impossible in any case, is made almost ridiculous by the fact that he has no say on matters of national policy. These are the province of the elected Representatives and Senators— who, however, do not necessarily agree among themselves, or even with the heads of the party in their states. The chairman of the national committee is thus faced with the unenviable assignment of inspiring the Republican organization to greater efforts, without being able to say anything authoritative about the party's interpretation of the issues.

Baffling as this may be to the well-disciplined European, it is an arrangement that serves freedom well. As was pointed out in "The System," the American political structure is not parliamentarian. The President is not responsible to the Congress, nor is his Cabinet. He is responsible directly to the people, but he is held accountable for his actions only once every four years. He may, consequently, retain in power Cabinet officers who do not have the confidence of the people. In the meantime

Congress may—and frequently does—become hostile to him as well as to members of his Cabinet.

This governmental system has its virtues, but it is characterized by a certain rigidity. If the American parties were divided into a party of the left and a party of the right, the result would be violent swings of policy as the powerful office of Chief Executive changed hands. Moreover, owing to the fact that Cabinet officers are appointed, no such thing as a coalition government is possible in the U.S. This was illustrated in 1940 when President Roosevelt appointed the Republican Henry L. Stimson as Secretary of War and the Republican Frank Knox as Secretary of the Navy. The move was theoretically shrewd, designed to enlist Republican support for the Roosevelt preparedness measures. But as soon as Messrs. Stimson and Knox accepted the Roosevelt bid they lost their power within their own party—indeed, in a fit of somewhat childish pique, the Republican leaders "read them out" of it. Were the conventional right-left split to give rise to several parties, under this rigid system orderly government would become almost impossible. Whichever party won, the presidency would win *all* the executive power, even though it represented only a small plurality of the voters.

Since flexibility is not provided by the American governmental structure, it has to be provided by the parties themselves. Each party must have—and under healthy conditions always has had—a "right" wing and a "left" wing. The reason why the Democratic party appears to be the party of the "left" is that under Franklin Roosevelt the progressive or "liberal" wing of the party (the

New Deal) won power within the party, and thereafter dictated the party's policies. It did not, however, eliminate the right wing of the party, which struggled against the New Deal throughout Roosevelt's administration, and which is still struggling—and even gaining ground. The situation within the Republican party is precisely the opposite. Here the conservative wing has been dominant. The progressive wing, however, has not been eliminated —indeed, with Wendell Willkie, it succeeded in capturing for a time the leadership of the party.

It is through this internal struggle that the American political party achieves its highest function, namely, that of national integration. The U.S., as has been so often pointed out in this book, is a diverse land, with many different sectional interests competing against each other, many different popular groups, many racial strains. In terms of pure political theory all this should be integrated in the Congress, where the people are officially represented. In practice it does not work out that way. For the most part, the Congress solves these conflicts through log-rolling, trading off one interest against the other, and sometimes yielding to overwhelming pressure. The political party, on the other hand, integrates in a positive way. To survive as a national party it must enlist the loyalty of at least a minority of every group in every section. These organizational minorities all have a common purpose: to win power at election time. To this end sectional interests may have to be subordinated within the party. It must nominate leaders and formulate policies that the people will follow. And in doing so it integrates a vast number of conflicting interests in an organic way.

Thus, the American political party has evolved into an almost ideal instrument for the type of government that Americans have chosen to adopt. To compensate for the inherent rigidity of that government, it has enormous flexibility. When in power it must carry the burden of national policy. When out of power its flexibility enables it to do a great deal of experimenting. It is possible for California, for example, to over-indulge (under a Republican governor) in state pensions and social security, without committing the whole party to an advocacy of the resulting deficits. Successful experiments are copied in other states and finally become official doctrine.

The weakness of the American political party, on the other hand, is the logical complement of its strength. The very fact that it is primarily an organization of men and women bent on seizing power and patronage leads to almost intolerable abuses. This is especially true, as Lord Bryce noted, in the large cities, where the party machines, relieved of any responsibility toward national or even state policies, are free to go their own way as pure power organizations. Such political machines exist to win votes—and for almost literally nothing else. Corruption under those circumstances is inevitable. Then, in the national elections, the vote-getting power of the machines is used to amass votes for a presidential candidate, who is thus forced to tolerate among his own supporters a level of political morality which, were he to practice it himself, would result in his impeachment.

Even where actual machines are absent, the emphasis of the American party system tends to fall much too heavily on vote-getting at the expense of matters of principle. One result is that local leadership deteriorates in character, and with it the caliber of political debate. Orators resort to a kind of emotional symbolism, hurling at the opposite party charges that could not possibly be substantiated, even if anyone knew what they really meant. The standard Republican attack on the Democrats as "socialists" is a case in point. On the other side, labor's attack on the Taft-Hartley Act as a "slave labor law" is for the most part equally emotional.

The result of these abuses has been a decline in the prestige of both parties and what looks like a rise in the size of the "independent" vote. In the 1950 election, for example, the people of New York City voted in overwhelming majorities for a Republican Governor, a Democratic Senator, and a Mayor who was running on a hastily concocted Experience party ticket all by himself. Connecticut elected two Democratic Senators and a Republican Governor. Ohio elected a Republican Senator and a Democratic Governor. And so forth. Increasingly, people are complaining that the parties are corrupt, that they are not needed anyway, and that if they want to survive they must choose better leaders.

To be sure, people who make this complaint are not always clear as to what they mean. It is plain foolishness to advocate, as many ill-informed Americans do, a rearrangement of the parties along doctrinaire lines. As already pointed out, both parties accept a set of principles and beliefs, referred to earlier as the Proposition and the

System. The idea that one party could be for the Proposition and the other party against the Proposition would signal the end of American democracy as it has thus far developed. The task of the political parties, on the contrary, is to apply the Proposition, to concern themselves with its evolution, to reinterpret it courageously and with imagination. When either party deviates too far from this course, it is sure to fall.

What the critics of the parties really mean—or, at any rate, what they ought to mean—is something different. The parties have fallen into disrepute, not because they lack issues, but because they have failed to provide moral leadership. The constant temptation for candidates and officeholders is to listen to the counsels of compromise and political expediency—to mention nothing worse—that emanate constantly from the "organization crowd." The American people are so fed up with this that they will flock by the million to the support of candidates who dare to defy their own organization. The case of Mayor Impellitteri of New York City is a spectacular example; and in Pennsylvania, James Duff, who challenged and overthrew the Grundy machine, was swept into the Senate by an overwhelming majority. Yet outright defiance of the organization is not necessary. The people will follow a man who has moral convictions and who is not afraid to utter them. In 1950 Senator Taft was even able to capture some of the labor vote, which was supposedly solid against him, because he stood uncompromisingly for his principles.

A study of the American political parties thus brings us out in approximately the same place as a study of the

American labor movement. Fixed doctrines and ideologies are lacking. Such doctrines, which in Europe provide a skeletal structure for domestic politics, are replaced in the U.S. by a system or framework which appears arbitrary in nature, but is in fact organic—for the good reason that the people have made it so. This framework is designed to serve *all* interests. And, like the labor movement, its present problem is leadership. Perhaps, in a middle-class society, this must always be so.

Moral leadership in political affairs, at any rate, is the peculiar and pressing obligation of the American political party, transcending even parliamentary leadership. An American party must be prepared to nominate and back men who have beliefs, and who have also the courage and skill to convince others of their validity. For it is by such beliefs, sometimes reached through great struggle, sometimes uttered at great political risk, that the American Proposition has been successfully implemented, generation after generation. And deep in their hearts the American people know that it is only in this way, and through the courage of such men, that the Proposition can endure and flourish.

THE BUSY,
BUSY CITIZEN

with a Note on A.A.

THE WORD democracy, which is used carelessly enough in our time, is usually taken to denote a certain type of political structure, the purpose of which is to provide for self-government by the people concerned. And yet it is almost a truism of political theory, and especially obvious in America, that politics and self-government are not by any means the same. The genius of American politics is one thing; the genius of American self-government, another. The latter certainly includes the former, but it also includes much else besides—for example, cultural and moral criteria, without which no people can hope to govern themselves.

One element of American self-government, which plays a role so vast as to be virtually immeasurable, has been relatively neglected by students of this country, whether foreign or domestic. It has been so little explored, indeed, that it is difficult to find a name for it. In lieu of a single name let us, therefore, quote a single man. "There are times," said Walter H. Wheeler, Jr., President of Pitney-Bowes of Stamford, Connecticut, "as I sit behind a desk piled high with the day's unread correspondence, when I stare darkly out of the window. Trying to see me are three conscientious executives, who would like to remind me, if they dared, that we're in business to make a profit, and that I must spend *some* time on the problem of sales, manufacturing, and development. There is a Community Chest meeting in five minutes, and a directors' meeting tomorrow morning, neither of which I am prepared for. I am supposed to make a talk before the American Management Association in two days, and I haven't started to think of what I shall say . . . At times like this I dream of establishing a Society for the Advancement of Irresponsible Businessmen . . . And yet, as if to personally prove the obstinate nature of man, I go on talking about our new responsibilities whenever I get the opportunity . . . It seems to me that none of us can look forward with hope over the years unless all of us can find solutions to problems bigger than our immediate material progress."

Every American man-of-affairs will recognize Mr. Wheeler's complaint. For if the world at large has the idea that the businessmen of the U.S.—or, for that matter, the American people generally—are wholly absorbed in their business and personal affairs, then the world is wrong. The truth is that Americans are just about as busy with their nonofficial, unremunerated, voluntary activities as they are with their official duties; and these unpaid, unofficial, off-duty activities have a deeper and more lasting effect upon American life, and even American policies, than do the official ones. In their official capacities Americans are busy businessmen, busy lawyers, busy politicians, workers, soldiers, teachers, housewives, etc.; but, when one has described all of that, one has still not touched the unique nerve of American life, which constantly stimulates initiative and at the same time makes these people truly "self-governed." American self-government, in short, is only partially achieved by the political parties. A great part of it—from certain aspects, the major part of it—stems from the voluntary activities of private citizens.

The tradition is a long one and was noted by Tocqueville more than a hundred years ago. "If an American were condemned to confine his activities to his own affairs," said that sage observer of the U.S., "he would feel robbed of half of his existence." The native urge for self-government bursts the bounds of official channels and spills over into all kinds of schemes for the improvement of the community, of one's self, of one's fellow man.

By and large, the more successful a man is, the more numerous and far-reaching are the obligations that he feels it necessary to recognize. At the very top of the ladder, wealthy capitalists have started foundations, some of whose assets reach as high as nine figures. In this category a pioneer was Andrew Carnegie, who began before the turn of the century to convert his huge gains into philanthropy—the Carnegie Corp. of New

York, the Carnegie libraries distributed all over the land, the research projects, the fellowships, and the scholarships, etc., to which he gave some $300 million. Mr. Carnegie, indeed, developed a theory of beneficent capitalism, which, while it would sound obsolete today, has had a profound effect on the evolution of American capitalistic ideas, as set forth in the chapter on that subject. Others were Sage and Duke, who set up sizable foundations; and, notably, the John D. Rockefellers, senior and junior, who together have given away three-quarters of a billion dollars. Alfred P. Sloan Jr., of General Motors, has his Sloan Foundation for the encouragement of an understanding of economic enterprise. And the Ford family has set up a huge half-billion-dollar foundation for "the advancement of the ideals and principles of democracy," with Paul G. Hoffman at the head of it.

Yet the big foundations, dedicated to various humanitarian goals, account for only a small fraction of the "public-spirited" activities in which Americans engage. Such a man as Thomas J. Watson, head of International Business Machines, for example, does not content himself with giving money away; the list of organizations to which he belongs occupies a full column in *Who's Who* and includes an almost incredible assortment of activities having to do with foreign affairs, art, music, religion, education, etc. Philip Reed, Chairman of the General Electric Co., is almost entirely concerned with a form of "statesmanship" that leads him into the International Chamber of Commerce, CED, and ECA—all of which has only a remote bearing upon the profit-and-loss statement of General Electric. And so on, down the line. In every city and town in America the leading businessmen consider it necessary to donate a large portion of their time to public activities for which they receive no remuneration.

In fact, it is often true that a young man starting off in a big company earns his promotions, not merely through proficiency in his job, but through his work in various community affairs, which results in a certain reputation and prestige that the "boss" cannot disregard. A young assistant in some department of a big company may, for example, become assistant campaign manager for the Community Chest Fund. He gets a special dispensation from management to give the fund his time, and if the drive is successful, he is in line for campaign manager at some future date—a job that brings him into contact with every important citizen of the community. There are rather definite limits, however, to which such a young man should venture. He should not become involved in anything too "political"; this might cause his company "embarrassment." This is one reason why American politics seems so short of able young men; and why, to get things done politically, Americans turn so often, and so hopefully, to extracurricular channels.

But all this activity and taking of responsibility is not by any means the prerogative of the leading industrialists. It runs right down into the smallest villages. There are at least 200,000 organizations, associations, clubs, societies, lodges, and fraternities in the U.S., along with innumerable social groups and *ad hoc* committees formed for specific causes. Except for the few intellectuals who don't believe in "joining," and the very, very poor who can't afford to, practically all adult Americans belong to some club or other, and most of them take part in some joint effort to do good. This prodigious army of volunteer citizens, who take time from their jobs and pleasure to work more or less unselfishly for the betterment of the community, is unique in the world. It is, in a way, the mainspring as well as the safeguard of democracy. For, whatever the silly rituals and earnest absurdities of some of their organizations, and the self-interest of others, the volunteers are always ready to work and fight for what they think is right.

Some of the organizations are primarily pressure groups—certain business, farm, labor, and veterans' organizations, for example—but they manage to do a lot of research and educational work too. Often, at the local level, they take on a share of the civic and charitable burden. In addition, there are countless organizations dedicated to the betterment of the community—the so-called "service" clubs, such as Rotary, Kiwanis, Lions, and local luncheon clubs of various kinds. The motives of the members, who meet, eat, and sing every week, may be selfish, in the sense that this mixing with other businessmen in the town is good for one's individual business; but at the same time these organizations do help to uphold standards of business ethics and carry out specific programs for the less privileged—to promote, as the Kiwanians put it, "righteousness, justice, patriotism, and good will." The fraternal orders—Moose, Elks, Eagles, Odd Fellows, etc.—are mutual-benefit societies and social clubs, but they also enter into local fund-raising campaigns and charitable projects.

The 1,350,000 members of the 17,000 clubs grouped together in the General Federation of Women's Clubs are into everything, of course, with their music and art and literature committees, study, education, and legislative groups, better-community campaigns and general uplift and do-goodness. When the lady delegates to a state or national convention pass a resolution urging the repeal of the law against yellow margarine or favoring federal aid to education, legislators pay attention. They pay even more attention to the smaller but politically more acute League of Women Voters; few candidates dare refuse to speak at league nonpartisan rallies.

Men may join an organization for business or political reasons, or because they find security in belonging to a group, or because they believe in accepting responsibility. They have learned that their own welfare rests in the welfare of all, and they contribute not only money to ameliorate misfortune, but brains and time to solve problems that reach far beyond old-fashioned charities. But their activities are by no means confined to "charity," "education," or community development; they break over into outright political causes, many of which have had a profound effect upon national policy. For example, the ill-fated prohibition law, which required an actual amendment to the Constitution, was brought about in large part by the work of the Anti-Saloon League. More successful—almost, it might be said, indispensable to the survival of the free world—was the William Allen White Committee to Defend America by Aiding the Allies, which in 1940 recognized the international danger while the country was in an isolationist mood, and which was followed by the spectacular and effective Fight for Freedom. The efforts of these and similar organizations literally changed the temper of the U.S. and enabled Franklin Roosevelt to prepare (just in time) for World War II. Similar organizations are springing up today—notably the Committee on the Present Danger, founded by a group of distinguished citizens for the purpose of galvanizing the people—and the government—into action. Others have more limited political ends. Many a candidate for the U.S. Senate or other high office owes his election primarily to "independent" committees formed for the specific purpose of electing him.

Thus the ordinary citizen's off-duty activities may include working for the removal of the billboard at the corner of Elm and Sixth, raising money for a new gym at the high school, campaigning for a city-manager plan, serving on the board of the State Health Council, fulfilling his duties as a member of the Rotary and the Chamber of Commerce, the Symphony Society and the hospital board, and giving time and money to such organizations as World Federalists, the Committee on the Present Danger, the Independent Committee to elect so-and-so to the Senate. All this goes on in addition to the job for which he is paid.

And his wife, the much-caricatured Madam Chairman, belongs to at least as many organizations, spends at least as much time on voluntary jobs, and much more time than her husband on lectures, study, self-improvement.

If she is a successful businessman's wife, she has her favorite charity (the Children's Home, perhaps, or the Visiting Nurse Association); she belongs to the Arts and Literature Committee of the Woman's Club, the Daughters of the American Revolution, and the Garden Club; she is a patroness of the Fine Arts Academy and the Little Theatre, and a charter member of the Wednesday Shakespeare Society. Her married daughter is active in the Parent-Teacher Association, Planned Parenthood, and the League of Women Voters; a member of the Junior League and the Vassar Club, and chairman this year of the Community Chest's North Side division.

The number of meetings held every day and week and month by these volunteer groups is uncountable. In each of the last few years there were something like 17,000 conventions in the U.S.—national, regional, and state, but *not* counting district or local. They were attended by ten million delegates, who spent about $1 billion. In Atlantic City in 1949, for example, about 240,000 delegates went to 250 conventions, including those of Optimist International, the Improved Order of Red Men, the Tall Cedars of Lebanon (Supreme Forest), and the New Jersey Association of Cemetery Officials. The average delegate stayed a little more than four days and spent $22.37 a day. At these gatherings the delegates not only passed resolutions affecting, to great or small degree, the policies of the country, but listened to speeches and discussions on world politics, freedom, and other subjects remote from business. Many went home resolved to work harder than ever in and for their own communities.

The number of meetings is equaled only by the number of dollars raised and spent. The two million volunteer workers who pound the sidewalks for U.S. Community Chests raised $193 million in 1949. Other thousands raised $110 million for United Jewish Appeal, $68 million for the Red Cross, $30 million for the National Foundation for Infantile Paralysis—altogether about $3 billion for philanthropy.

All these people may put more effort into lunches and speech-making and Be It Resolveds than into getting the job done. Often their work is uncoordinated and overlapping. Often groups split apart on minor ideologies and thus defeat the major project. And lately the witch-hunting element of anti-Communism may have dampened innocent idealism in some instances. But by and large throughout the land the leading citizen still devotes his time and energy to civic betterment. Madam Chairman still presides with authority and purity of purpose. And the humble member of the club still faithfully performs his "duty of mutual help owed by man to man."

Yet the mere enumeration of all these activities cannot reveal their true significance to American life. The real meaning and effectiveness of off-duty organizations can be understood only at the community level, where they weave themselves into an organic pattern and become to a great extent mutually interdependent.

Literally any American community might be chosen to illustrate what citizenship in this sense really means.

136

We turn, quite arbitrarily, to Cedar Rapids, Iowa, a thriving midwestern city of 72,149 people intent on making democracy work.

Most of the people of Cedar Rapids are comfortably well off, living in modest frame houses on shaded streets. A few are rich; a few are poor. There are enough good jobs and opportunities in the well-diversified industries to keep most of the young men at home. It is traditional for the men in industry, banking, retailing, even journalism, to assume a share of responsibility for the community—"paying our civic rent" is a favorite slogan. There are 372 organizations in town, counting labor unions and religious groups, but not counting hundreds of social and specialty clubs such as the Ladies Literary, the Gladiolus, the Merimyx Dancing, the Bird and Natural Science, and the Society for the Preservation and Encouragement of Barber Shop Quartet Singing.

On Monday at noon Rotary meets at the Roosevelt. On Tuesday the Optimists (the ladies' auxiliary is called the Opti-Mrs. Club) eat at the Roosevelt, Exchange and Canopus at the Montrose; Kiwanis at the Roosevelt on Wednesday; the Lions on Thursday; Hi-Twelve (Masonic) on Friday. These "service" clubs, with members from each profession and retail group, go through a lot of backslapping and singing of *K-K-K-Katie,* but they also bring fellowship and a certain amount of dignity to ordinary businessmen. Most of the clubs have projects such as helping crippled children, sponsoring 4-H clubs, or raising money to support the six European students now attending local schools and colleges.

The Ancient & Honorable Society of Free & Accepted

137

Masons is strong, with some 3,200 men, important and unimportant, initiated to the mystic rites. There are 1,800 members of the Benevolent & Protective Order of Elks (a few of whom belong for the sole privilege of being allowed to buy drinks at the Elks Club in dry Cedar Rapids); Moose, Eagles, Odd Fellows, Red Men, Knights of Columbus, Knights of Pythias, and members of the Dramatic Order of Knights of Khorasan (the Dokies). Most lodges indulge in charitable enterprises as well as medieval ritual. They vary in appeal to different economic and social levels and there are enough of them to provide a rallying point for every man in town.

The American Legion membership in Cedar Rapids, as elsewhere, includes businessmen, lawyers, politicians, white-collar men, and laborers. Hanford Post (3,300 members) is fighting now for rent control, veterans' housing, the rehabilitation of veterans, and universal military training. "If we want something," boasts commander John Baldridge, "we generally get it." Schoolbooks, Baldridge says, ought to be full of what a wonderful place America is, but instead they are full of Communism. All Communists ought to be put in prison. Baldridge believes the little fellow ought to be heard more in the nation's councils; in fact, he's getting sort of interested in politics himself. He thinks the United Nations is "a fine project— but they do too much talking."

On the morning of October 24, 1950, twenty-five women met in the Little Theatre in the basement of the Y.M.C.A. to observe United Nations Day. The meeting was sponsored by the Council of Church Women and the Radio

Council. Mrs. F. E. Corey presided. "The U.N.," she said, "is one of the biggest things in our personal lives today. We hope a branch of the Association for the U.N. will be started in Cedar Rapids."

Mrs. Carl Ettinger, active member of the American Association of University Women, described her impressions of a recent visit to Lake Success. She and Mr. Ettinger were fortunate because the woman in charge of admissions happened to be an Iowan, too, and got them into the delegates' lounge. They stood quite close to Vishinsky and Malik and Acheson and talked to Mrs. Edith Sampson. "You would all be proud of her." In the Assembly the recognition of Communist China was being discussed. It was cut and dried. But in the lounge and the cafeteria "it was very democratic and the spirit of camaraderie was heartening."

Mrs. Corey listed the U.N. radio programs that could be heard in town and passed out U.N. literature to be distributed to the forty member clubs of the council. The city was at fault, she said, for not planning to observe U.N. Day. She herself went to nine stores and they all agreed to have window displays of posters. Catholic churches were planning to ring bells at eleven, and other churches and schools that had bells would ring them, too. "It will be through prayer and the United Nations that we may hope for World Peace."

On November 12 and 13 the American Friends Service Committee, along with St. Paul's Church, Coe College, the Y.M.C.A., Y.W.C.A., the Cedar Rapids Federation of Labor, Council of Church Women, Camp Fire Girls, D.A.R., A.A.U.W., Junior League, Rotary, Woman's

Club, and Chamber of Commerce, sponsored a two-day Conference on World Questions to "stimulate community thinking on the problems of peace."

The club women, more than the men, talk and work for peace. They listen to lectures by college professors, war correspondents, and "world travelers"; they read books by John Foster Dulles, James Burnham, Winston Churchill, and Peter Drucker; they study assigned subjects such as "The Unification of Western Europe," "The Marshall Plan at Work," "Can the World Be Changed?"; they read papers and pass resolutions. "We're sort of conservative here," says Mrs. Lester L. Johnson, president of the Woman's Club (550 members). "We wait and see —don't jump into radical causes. During the war we didn't have any pacifist or militaristic groups.* We just sort of went along with the war effort." (As a matter of fact, Cedar Rapids more than "went along." Among other things, it bought so many war bonds so early that it was the first U.S. city to receive the Treasury's "T.")

At a League of Women Voters meeting on the night of October 24, more than a hundred men and women listened to five congressional and state candidates. The questions asked after the speeches, on U.N. support, money for peace, soldiers' bonus, state aid to schools, and "socialized" medicine, were intelligent and in some cases embarrassing to the candidates. The league, fairly new in Cedar Rapids, is made up of young, active women who

---

* Verne Marshall of Cedar Rapids, former editor of the *Gazette,* was the stormy head of the No Foreign Wars Committee in 1940, is now in semi-retirement but devotes a lot of time to supporting the foreign students in town.

keep informed on current legislation and voting records, work hard for their principles.

Many of these same women and some of their husbands are among the 3,000 members of the local council of the P.T.A. who attend study groups for parents and leadership training courses, work for the better health and welfare of the school children, the improvement of the schools, democracy, and tolerance. (One of their best unit presidents last year was a colored woman, Mrs. Robert Atkinson.) "Education," says the President, Mrs. John Mathews, "is our best hope of peace."

The Chamber of Commerce, which includes the Junior Chamber in its Young Men's Bureau, is the organization that really runs Cedar Rapids. Each of its 2,300 members serves on one or more of the bureaus, committees, and subcommittees. At a typical board meeting eighteen of the twenty-one members were on hand Friday noon in a private dining room of the Roosevelt Hotel. These men were the busy executives, bankers, lawyers of Cedar Rapids. Not one of them looked or talked like George Follansbee Babbitt of Sinclair Lewis' Zenith. From twelve to twelve-thirty (sharp) they ate breaded veal cutlets, mashed potatoes, green salad, mince pie, and coffee. President Keith Dunn (Executive Vice President of Century Engineering Co.) called the meeting to order and the executive secretary, Bob Caldwell, read the minutes and reported that the General Fund's $1,905 deficit for the first nine months would be wiped out by the end of the year. Mr. Dunn said that at the next meeting he would like to have the board consider raising the dues above the current $30 a year.

Van Vechten Shaffer, President of the Guaranty Bank & Trust Co., chairman of the chamber's coordinating committee, reviewed the work of the Retired Men's Bureau, Retail Merchants' Bureau, and Wholesalers' Bureau. "Something," he said, "has to be done about those wholesalers."

Mr. Shaffer (this time in the role of member of the Public Welfare Bureau) reported that Sadie Palmer had left $53,000 to the Community Chest, but since the chest is part of the chamber and not a legal entity he wanted to put the money in trust, in the Peoples' Bank, not his Guaranty Trust or board member John Hamilton's Merchants—that might look funny. There were no objections.

There was informal talk about a new industry that was nibbling at the chamber's bait. Shortage of labor was the hitch—and that was due largely to shortage of housing. That's the real problem.

At one-forty-five, there being no further business, the meeting adjourned. President Dunn hurried to the next dining room to get in on the tail end of a Community Chest Fund meeting (the fund was still $5,000 short of its $216,000 goal); from there he was going to judge a parade at local Coe College. "When I get back to my own business," he said, "it seems like a vacation."

Work for the Chamber of Commerce is only one activity of most of the members. Mr. Shaffer, for example, gives at least a third of his time, often more, to the community. He feels the city wouldn't be worth living in if its citizens didn't work for it. Aside from his Chamber of Commerce duties, he is a trustee and secretary of Coe College, president of the Cedar Rapids Community Foundation, chairman of the local Health Council, member of the Iowa Health Council, and on its legislative committee. "All these things probably help my business, but that isn't why I do them."

Shaffer helped raise money for St. Luke's Hospital and gives to many charities and institutions and to the local symphony and the amateur theatre (the Footlighters). He resigned from Kiwanis because he didn't want to spare a lunch hour every week. He never joined the Masons, as his father and grandfather did. "In those days there weren't many social outlets here; I don't need the Masons or Elks for a social life." Shaffer is a strong believer in eliminating waste and coordinating civic effort. "You can really organize in a town this size where everyone knows what everyone else is doing." During the war he helped amalgamate all related agencies into a War Chest that became the model for many other cities. And he thinks the next big job to be done in Cedar Rapids is to make a survey of all charities and civic work and get rid of unnecessary or overlapping committees and boards. He grumbles sometimes about the many things he is expected to do. "When Caldwell calls from the chamber to ask me to take on another job, I say 'Why damn it, Bob'— but I'll be there to do it."

A different kind of leader in Cedar Rapids is Howard Hall, President of Iowa Manufacturing (road-building machinery) and Iowa Steel & Iron. He is no joiner and takes no outward part in civic life. He says he makes his contribution to Cedar Rapids by running his companies well and providing jobs, but others go to him for counsel and behind-the-scenes action as well as for contributions to their causes. Right now, for instance, when the chamber is trying to lure a new industry to town and skilled labor is tight, Hall has offered to lend a force of his machinists to get the new company started. Once violently anti-union, he changed his mind after a bad strike at his own Iowa Manufacturing in 1936. He and Clare Blodgett, A.F. of L. spokesman and editor of the labor weekly, serve together on a labor-management committee that has helped guarantee stability and given assurance of labor peace to prospective new industry.

More typical of Cedar Rapids businessmen than Howard Hall is Sutherland Dows, president of the Iowa Electric Light & Power Co. Mr. Dows is, naturally, a member of the Chamber of Commerce and he serves on its New Housing and Industries committees, its All-Iowa Fair Association, and Greater Cedar Rapids Fund. He is chairman of the board of trustees of Cornell College in nearby Mount Vernon, a member of the Coe College executive and finance committees, chairman of the trustees of Camp Good Health, trustee of the Oak Hill Cemetery Association, a director of the Executives Club, and a trustee of the Midwest Research Institute. He has served on the boards of the Y.M.C.A., First Presbyterian Church, Salvation Army, St. Luke's Hospital, Boy Scouts Regional Committee, Community Chest, and City Plan Commission. He is still a member of the Masons, the Elks, the American Legion, the Veterans of Foreign Wars, the

Cedar Rapids Country Club, the Pickwick, the University Club of Chicago, the Milwaukee Club of Milwaukee.

Mr. Dows is a director or officer of sixteen companies besides his own, has served as delegate to the Republican county and state conventions for a number of years; he frequently addresses women's clubs and civic groups on local history (his hobby); when he is in town he lunches at the Roosevelt with the Horsebuyers, a small group of businessmen who discuss affairs of the day informally. And, somehow, he manages to find time to run Iowa E.L.&P., a company with 1,300 employees and $62 million in assets.

The president of Smulekoff's big furniture store, A. L. Smulekoff, figures that he gives between a third and a half of his time to civic affairs. "I was brought up to serve the community." He can't remember all the organizations he belongs to; most of his time now is spent trying to unite the different Jewish groups in town and working for St. Luke's (Methodist) Hospital. Unlike many retail merchants, he approves the recent credit regulations ("The National Retail Credit Association thinks I'm a nut") because he is deeply concerned with the seriousness of the international situation. He talks about foreign affairs instead of Big Ten football, and when he is in New York spends his leisure at Lake Success instead of at *South Pacific* or *Kiss Me, Kate.*

Another retailer in town, Robert Armstrong, president of Armstrong Clothing, was brought up, like Mr. Smulekoff, to take responsibility in the community. And he, too, is interested in America's foreign policies. "There are very few isolationists here," he says. "Easterners just think so because of the Chicago *Tribune*." Armstrong is president of the board of St. Luke's. A few years ago he led a successful campaign to get higher salaries for Cedar Rapids teachers. And like most of the other leaders in town he gives substantial donations to worthy causes; in fact, he follows the tithing rule and contributes 10 per cent of his income to charity. In addition, the firm contributes 5 per cent of its profits.

There are at least a dozen other businessmen who do about as much as these five.

The volunteer activities of Cedar Rapids go on and on. No report on them can be complete, because the over-all task that they undertake is infinite. It is the task of citizenship—full citizenship in a society that still believes that the role of government should be held to a minimum and the role of the individual should be encouraged to expand. A modern society has a heavy social load to bear. Things are always getting out of adjustment, people are always in trouble, reforms are always needed, new ideas and new causes are always begging for attention. What proportion of the total social load of America is borne by voluntary activities such as we have described, it is of course impossible to know. But those who know America best know that it is enormous; that with all the billions spent by government on social problems and public welfare, the government share of the total, measured in terms of human energy and perseverance, is only a tiny fraction. Americans are a self-governing people, not just politically but also socially.

146

This is a phenomenon of great importance to the maintenance of the American System. And it is a phenomenon that opens for America—and perhaps eventually for the free world—vast new possibilities in the field of social management. That aspect of the matter is developed in "Individualism Comes of Age," Chapter IX, where an American solution to the problem of state socialism is proposed, and to some extent documented. The people of Cedar Rapids, pursuing the ramified obligations of American citizenship, are part of the documentation.

A Note on Alcoholics Anonymous

The tremendous efforts expended by Americans on social problems in their private capacities may be viewed at the community level, as we have just seen in connection with Cedar Rapids, Iowa. Or they may be viewed at the national level through the study of a single organization. Both views are necessary to a comprehension of the whole phenomenon. We append, therefore, a note on an organization which is certainly not "typical"—indeed, it is unique—but which illustrates certain native American characteristics that provide a basic soil for voluntary social activity of all sorts.

Alcoholics Anonymous was conceived by a drunk lying on a bed in a drunks' hospital in New York in 1934, and had a hard birth in Akron, Ohio, the following year. A doctor of medicine was present, but at this critical moment was too alcoholically jittery to know an accouchement was taking place. The American tradition

147

of adverse beginnings was thus fulfilled by this organization, which today equally fulfills the tradition of success
after struggle. By birthplace, heritage, tradition, habits,
looks, and tone of voice Alcoholics Anonymous is unmistakably American. And yet in almost every way it con-
tradicts the stencils by which non-American minds gauge
American achievement. It has almost no money and
wishes it could do with still less. In fifteen years its membership has grown from nothing to 120,000, yet it never
urges anyone to join. Of formal "organization" it has almost none, yet it avers it "ought never to have any." A
man or woman becomes a member by simple declaration,
and need share his decision with only one other human
being. There are no pledges or constraints in A.A.; no
records that must be kept or quotas that must be broken.
Seniority confers no favors. A.A. has one purpose only:
"to help the sick alcoholic recover, *if he wishes.*"

In a world whose spiritual values have dropped close
to the vanishing point, the strange society of A.A. bases
its entire proposition upon the reality of spiritual experience. It achieves harmony among a membership in which
Catholics associate not only with Protestants and Jews
but with high-decibel agnostics or fancy religionists of
species known only to God. Its members, who know better than to contradict the psychiatrists' diagnosis that
they are "grandiose, infantile, and self-absorbed," practice daily an Obedience that has no enforcement mechanism and no system of punishment for infraction. The
one rule common to every A.A. clubhouse is that if, as
rarely occurs, a member seeks to attend a meeting while

drinking, he is escorted to the door, with the invitation to return only as soon as he recalls his society's purpose.

If A.A., successful and American, had a password proof against any member's forgetting, it would be "Failure." One by one, each member tackled something that proved too big for him; only when he acknowledged his inability to deal with a circumstance that most people can meet with ease was he able to become a full member of this organization, of those for whom "one drink is too many and a thousand aren't enough." Dentists and doctors, stevedores, ministers, cops, poets, publishers, matrons, vocational-guidance counselors, stenographers, artists, bartenders, and master mechanics are all to be found in A.A.'s ranks, as diverse and exclusive as a classified telephone directory. Yet all have a common vantage point; each one, from a broad and comfortable ridge, has a clear view downward into the Valley of the Shadow of Death.

Although alcoholism is a state so complex that a leak-proof definition is impossible here, a clinician can, in his own bald terms, describe it simply: "a progressive, incurable and fatally terminating disease." That alcoholism could be *arrested* was well known, but this knowledge was for many years almost useless, for the arrestment was up to the drinker: would he or would he not stop? Usually he would not, no matter how he longed to, for he was inwardly convinced that he could not; so long as he knew that a couple of quick ones would give him a desperately bought temporary relief from his sufferings, he could see no permanent way out. Psychiatry's dictum that alcoholism was only a symptom of a deep-seated psychic disorder was not very helpful in the crisis forever engulfing the alcoholic and his family.

It dawned on Bill W.* in 1934, when he was close to the last stages of alcoholic disintegration, that if he attempted to help other alcoholics he might thereby help himself. He went to work—and found himself able to stay sober for the first time in years. But this was cold comfort, for the drunks on whom he worked stayed drunk. He was on the verge of a relapse that might well have been final when he met the drunken Dr. Bob in Akron. Only then did it dawn that the help must flow two ways: one-sided preachment was useless, but when help was mutually offered and accepted between two suffering and desperate drunks, each of whom sought to help himself by helping the other, a new element entered into a materialistically hopeless situation. As a result of this help from the helpless, Bill W. stayed sober and Dr. Bob got sober, and the nucleus of Alcoholics Anonymous was formed. By the end of that year A.A. had three members. By the end of another year it had fifteen. By the end of still another it had forty—divided among Akron, New York, and Cleveland. That was all.

Since those years A.A. has evolved into a membership of 120,000 divided into some 4,100 local groups. Metropolitan areas such as New York, Cleveland, Chicago,

---

* Anonymity is, to the A.A., of immense spiritual significance—reminding him "to place principles above personalities." Bill W. and Dr. Bob, referred to in this article, were the first two members of A.A. and thus cannot escape some indentification as "founder" and "co-founder." Dr. Bob's death late in 1950 revealed him at last to the general public as Dr. Robert H. Smith, noted surgeon of Akron, Ohio.

and Los Angeles may harbor 100 to 200 groups each.*
Ninety prisons have A.A. clubs within their walls, and
over 100 clubs exist to further the A.A. idea, although
not formally affiliated with A.A. In Chicago the weekly
"intergroup" meeting never brings out fewer than 1,200
A.A.'s at a time. In New York, the "Annual Banquet" may
have to be abandoned unless some way can be devised of
splitting it into sections, for no hotel has a ballroom large
enough to seat it.

Much more important are the statistics of sobriety. Of
those who make a genuine effort to stop drinking through
A.A. principles, 50 per cent get sober at once, and stay
that way. Another 25 per cent get sober after some re-
lapses. The remaining 25 per cent show improvement.
A.A. is not out to make a showing. It refuses to screen its
membership, as some doctors would like, to eliminate
the "hopeless" cases; gaining a statistical advantage is
not A.A.'s purpose—and furthermore an impressive number of "hopeless" cases have recovered. A.A. quietly and
with good cause believes that all those who relapse or
drop away will be back later and permanently, if they
live. The word "cure," however, is not in the A.A. vocabulary. On the contrary, the man who succeeds in stay-
ing sober must still recognize himself as an alcoholic.

Suppose you were to go to an open meeting of A.A., as
you are perfectly free to do. You would find yourself in a
group of from thirty to 300 people, one-third of whom
might be women. (Only 10 to 15 per cent of A.A.'s active

---

* Of all groups needing A.A., the American Negro stands first. A.A. welcomes him, but the Negro's knowledge of alcoholism as a sickness is under-
standably slow in developing. Only in the last few years have A.A. groups
formed in Negro communities such as New York's Harlem.

membership is female, but non-alcoholic wives of alcoholic husbands are attending meetings in increasing numbers, and this attendance is strongly encouraged.) The average age would be between thirty-five and forty and is steadily growing younger; it used to be that an alcoholic seldom recognized his trouble until his middle forties, whereas now, with greater publicity for the whole problem, he sees what is wrong sooner; today, some A.A.'s are not much over thirty. Prosperous, less prosperous, and poor would be represented in about equal thirds; so would the educational levels of college, high school, or less. If this were a typical meeting, 40 per cent of those present would be Catholics—double the number you would encounter in an exact sample of the U.S. population. At the other end of the scale are the Jews—represented by no more than a sprinkling, even in New York.

There is no use trying to draw conclusions from appearances; the blowzy old lady near the front may be a casual visitor who never had a drink in her life, whereas the pink-cheeked, white-haired gentleman who looks like a deacon may have had a record of fifty alcoholic admissions into hospitals and jails. The group is probably meeting in the parish house of a church, a political clubhouse, a public auditorium, or a small mezzanine banquet room of a hotel—any place where an evening's rent is reasonable and the atmosphere is neither so high-toned as to discourage a man wearing out his last pair of shoes nor so forbidding as to scare a Caspar Milquetoast. The air is dense with tobacco smoke, and the evening's chairman has to bang his gavel hard to cut through the loud, familiar talk. There is no set speech for chairmen, but a typical opening might be something like this:

"Ladies and gentlemen, I wonder if the new people who are here for the first, second, or third time would please raise their hands. . . . That's fine. I'll ask the old-timers to please make themselves known to the new people and try to see they have a good time. As you know, A.A. groups have two kinds of meetings, open and closed. The closed meetings are for alcoholics only, but tonight is an open meeting, so everybody is welcome. If there are any reporters here I just want to remind them that they can write anything they like so long as they don't use anybody's name. You've got to respect us on that because some people are funny: they usen't to mind being seen in the Hotel Metropolis so drunk they couldn't stand up, but they're still a little bit sensitive about being seen sitting down here cold sober. . . .

"Maybe you think we have some fancy test that can tell you whether you're an alcoholic or not. But we haven't. The only person who can decide whether you're an alcoholic is yourself. If you want a little helpful hint I'll tell you something I heard Fanny J. say at a meeting a couple of months ago: when anybody stops *boasting* about how much he had to drink the night before and starts *lying* about it, there's maybe just a little bit of a chance that he's getting to be one of us. But that's up to you.

"Some people are able to get the A.A. program while they still have their jobs and their wives and their homes, but there are others who don't seem to be able to quit drinking until they've lost everything. That's given rise

153

to the saying that there are 'high-bottom' drunks and 'low-bottom' drunks. But remember what Bill W. said: 'The difference between the high-bottom drunk and the low-bottom drunk is that both are lying in the gutter but the high-bottom drunk has his head on the curb.' We are all drunks. If you think you are a drunk we invite you to join us.

"You're going to hear from three members tonight, and they're all going to have very different stories to tell. All we ask of you new people is that you keep an open mind. If you don't happen to hear anything tonight that fits in with your own story, or reminds you of your own pattern of drinking, please keep coming, for sooner or later you're bound to hear something that hits you right where you live.

"And I ought to tell the newcomers that we don't practice any religious ritual of any sort here, except that we end every meeting by standing up and reciting the Lord's Prayer, and we ask you all to join. The first speaker this evening . . ."

The first speaker, and every speaker at every A.A. meeting, begins with one standard line: "My name is ————, and I am an alcoholic." Thereafter he says exactly what he likes, and what he usually likes is to tell the story of his drinking, and how, eventually, he came into A.A. What a newcomer, feeling in his heart of hearts that he is an alcoholic, expects to experience at the first meeting can never be known, except it is a good bet he does not expect to be shaken with laughter. But that is what usually does happen to him, and what usually dissolves his intention of leaving after the first twenty minutes and making a dash for the nearest bar. No one has quite such terrific stories to tell as an alcoholic, and once he is released from his fears and shames by having put his alcoholic activity behind him he makes a formidable raconteur, using his old self as the butt of his new. The laughter that shakes the hall is the laughter of recognition.

Over and over, the newcomer hears references to the Twelve Steps and in particular to *the* Twelfth Step. The Twelve Steps constitute at once the philosophy of A.A. and its means to therapy for the alcoholic who is making an honest attempt to stop drinking. They are not absolutes, but are presented as *suggestions*. In condensed form for the quick-reading non-alcoholic, they are these:

First, the alcoholic admits that he has become powerless over alcohol; that his life has become unmanageable. This is the admission of failure without which his ego does not undergo the deep deflation that seems the key to success.

Next, he comes to believe that only a Power greater than himself can restore his life, and turns his will and his life over to the care of God *as he understands Him.*

Further, via nine detailed suggestions, the alcoholic undertakes a searching moral inventory of himself; admits to God and one human being his wrongs and shortcomings, asking God to remove them, and himself making the human amends possible. He seeks by prayer and meditation to improve his conscious contact with God as he understands Him, praying only for knowledge of His will, and the power to carry that out.

Finally, having had a spiritual experience, he tries to carry this message to alcoholics, and to practice these principles in all his affairs (the Twelfth Step).

"Alcoholics Anonymous," said Bill W. when the American Psychiatric Association invited him to address it in 1949, "is not a religious organization; there is no dogma. The one theological proposition is 'Power greater than one's self,' but even this concept is forced on no one. The newcomer merely immerses himself in our society and tries the program as best he can. Left alone, he will surely report the gradual onset of a transforming experience, call it what he may. Observers once thought A.A. could appeal only to the religiously susceptible. Yet our membership includes a former member of the American Atheist Society and about 20,000 others almost as tough. The dying can become remarkably open-minded. Of course we speak little of conversion nowadays because so many people really dread being God-bitten. But conversion, as broadly described by William James, does seem to be our basic process. . . .

"Our deep kinship, the urgency of our mission, the need to abate our neurosis for contented survival; all these, together with love for God and man, have contained us in surprising unity. There seems safety in numbers. Enough sandbags muffle any amount of dynamite. We think we are a pretty secure, happy family. Drop by any A.A. meeting for a look."

Among the toughest of the tough, the lowest of the low, the most cynical of the cynical, the program works. The alcoholic, man or woman, is merely urged to look again at the idea of a Higher Power, and to dissociate that idea from the old-man-with-the-whiskers, the angry Santa Claus, the avenging anthropomorphic tyrant with which he was stuffed and terrified in his childhood. Gradually the phrase "as *you* understand Him" takes hold. Sometimes the concept of the Higher Power can be accepted only by some elaborate stratagem. One alcoholic, determined in his agnosticism, at last solved his problem by accepting as a Power greater than himself the steam radiator that clanked and hissed in his miserable room. It was hot and full of energy and burned him when he touched it. It was sufficient. The radiator clanked inscrutably; the alcoholic stopped drinking.

One by one, the speakers who rise and tell their stories 12,000 times or more a week the country over are driven to say the same thing: "I don't understand it, but I don't need to; it works." Certainly one thing that works is the feeling of fellowship engendered by several hundred people in the same room, every one of whom knows at firsthand the exact horrible details of alcoholic suffering. Most alcoholics, before they encounter A.A., are convinced that nowhere in the annals of medicine or abnormal psychology can any parallel to themselves be found. "It may be all right for some people but it would never work for *me*" is the most common first response heard by an A.A. having his first talk with an alcoholic who does not yet dare to hope. Nothing is a more powerful solvent to this sort of suffering egotism than being physically surrounded by several hundred people, every one of whom once held precisely that same thought, and slowly realizing that the horrors once thought to be unique are, in reality, a universal experience in the society of A.A. Most A.A.'s carry fat address books in their pockets; in these are crammed the names, addresses, and telephone numbers of the A.A.'s he has met inside or outside his own group. This is the equipment he needs for what is known as the Nickel Therapy: when the desire for a drink reaches dangerous proportions, the A.A. drops a 5-cent piece in a coin telephone and dials the number of a fellow member who will sit out the siege with him.

The twelfth step, by which alcoholics work with alcoholics, does not mean that A.A. evangelizes, proselytizes, or whoops things up in any way among "hot prospects." If a despairing wife calls an A.A. (almost every sizable telephone book in the U.S. has an A.A. number in it) and asks that he "try to do something with Jim," the first inquiry must always be directed to the point, "Does Jim want it?" If the answer is "No, but God knows he ought to," the A.A. will beg off seeing Jim and have a chat with his wife or family instead. Only when Jim says he is ready to talk will the A.A. go to work directly. Even then, there is no urging. The A.A. member will talk not about Jim but about himself. He will emphasize that no A A. takes any sort of pledge of sobriety. He works, instead, on the "Twenty-four Hour Plan," which the A.A. often expresses as "Tomorrow I may go on the damnedest bender you ever heard of, but I'm not going to have a drink *today*." The Twenty-four Hour Plan is of vital importance to those who have newly stopped drinking— for to them, nine times out of ten, the contemplation of the balance of a lifetime without the solace of alcohol is intolerable. Yet A.A.'s who have been dry ten years or more still wisely make their plans for sobriety no further than a day in advance. The first longing of someone who has stopped drinking is to be able to resume it successfully; only slowly is this point of view replaced by the one that says "I wouldn't take a drink now, even if I could." All this the A.A. discusses at low pressure.

Where the A.A. truly burns to get something across to the suffering alcoholic is in telling him that not only is life *possible* without alcohol but it is a damned sight more pleasant. This is difficult. A universal feature of advanced alcoholism is a sharp constriction of interests: the alcoholic who once belonged to a choral society, went to sketch class once a week, collected matchbooks, and went on short-line railroad excursions has now abandoned all these things in favor of continuous drinking. It is hard for him to find his way back to these things alone: it is hard for him to find his way back to society at all. But A.A. offers him a society that will instantly welcome him, ask him no questions, but instead begin to deluge him with the mirthful, frightful record of its own calamities.

A.A. is founded on the Christian principle of Love. It is the fashion, even in these dark days, for the worldly to scoff at such a declaration, but the A.A. does not scoff and does not blush at holding so old-fashioned an idea. Like ceasing to drink, the A.A. finds that loving his fellow man makes no impossible exactions of an ordinary, all-too-human being. . . .

There was once a new A.A. named Joe, who came to

an older A.A. named Fred, asking advice. Joe had encountered a third A.A. named George whose every attribute of personality Joe found repulsive. Was it essential that Joe should love George? Yes, said Fred, it was. Joe thought for a long, dismal moment and then announced that if this were true he would have to retire from the program and resume drinking; loving George was beyond his powers.

"Wait a minute," said the old A.A. "There isn't anything to keep you from loving George. Hell, you don't have to *like* the s.o.b. any more than I do."

PART 3.

Having learned in the past how to apply their Proposition, Americans must now extend it into the future and into the world. In this part we face some long-range problems and venture some long-range projections.

viii

THE PROBLEMS
OF FREE MEN

with a Note on the Technological Revolution

THE FOUR preceding chapters have been concerned with four basic American institutions: capitalism, the labor movement, the political parties, and voluntary, private social activity. These four institutions were chosen for examination, not because they are in any sense inclusive, but because they represent excellent vantage points from which to view the action of the American Proposition upon the lives of free men and women. They offer good angles of observation, each for different reasons: capitalism, because the principles of the Proposition are bringing about a spectacular and little-understood transformation; labor, because those same principles have endowed it with a certain social stability that is hard to find elsewhere; the political parties, because these are the instruments through which the Proposition, while retained, is constantly modified; voluntary social activities, because, through these, the Proposition can speak without reference to government. All put together, fragmentary though they certainly are, they illustrate an amazing power of growth and change. This growth and change is animated by the general principles of the Proposition, which are embedded within the society in a dynamic way; and consequently, it has *direction*. Taken as a whole, what is going on in these areas strongly suggests that the U.S.A. is in process of developing new solutions to a number of the formidable socio-economic-political problems which, in modern times, have so shaken the institutions of free men.

This is not by any means to announce the millennium, however. When the American looks ahead toward the future he sees the possibility for the realization of great hopes; but he also and inevitably sees problems. Problems are of the essence of American life, because the American revolution is also an evolution, a process. Problems thus enter into the *meaning* of America in an intimate way; and since that is what we are primarily concerned with, it will be well to have a brief look at some of the major ones which Americans are facing—which are currently challenging (so to speak) the validity of the Proposition.

Americans do not like problems; yet they have a conscience about them, with the result that the most accurate criticism of their society has come, not from abroad, but from Americans themselves. Critics of American society, from Adams and Jefferson to Mencken and Steinbeck, have leveled telling charges at whatever they considered to be "wrong" with their country. And in response to these criticisms, Americans have repeatedly taken action. As pointed out in "The Busy, Busy Citizen," they rush to form innumerable committees, leagues, councils, and societies organized to cope with nearly everything, from World War III to such causes as that forwarded by the National Society to Discourage the Use of the Name Smith for Purposes of Hypothetical Illustration.

Today, all American problems are fatefully overshadowed by the problem—the possibility—of war. This, mankind's oldest plague, is what Americans most want to avoid, and only with the greatest reluctance do they admit that war, or the possibility of war, will continue as long as men will die for what they want. Whether what they want is loot or power, or the survival or spread of ideas and ideals, it is growing clear to many that war will remain until mankind is able somehow to put the ideal of internationalism above the idea of nationalism. Meanwhile, though the present crisis has temporarily eclipsed all other problems, their existence continues to alarm, madden, and sadden a great many Americans.

One of the American's characteristic errors is the assumption that human and social problems can be solved by one panacea or another, once and for all time. This is perhaps the oldest deception that man has practiced on himself. It is the deception responsible for all the utopias and the disillusion that they in turn have bred. The American Proposition itself is certainly not free of utopian overtones. But it contains within it one saving feature: its insistence on the freedom of men to work out their own freedom. This means—inevitably—problems. In fact, it is this freedom to experiment, to make mistakes and learn therefrom, that has produced the permanent American revolution.

Besides trying to fix them, Americans have created problems out of problems. Far from providing utopian solutions, freedom somehow manages to compound the difficulties. To cope with New York City's 1950 water shortage, for example, a cloud-seeding rain maker was hired, whose activities at once materialized the problem of one state's right to moisture that might naturally have fallen on another. This compounding of problems has resulted in a thunderous list, which confronts every American who has the courage and energy to give it his attention; which, indeed, is daily dinned into him by editorials, sermons, articles, speeches, books, plays, cartoons, paintings, and advertisements. It starts with war, defense, and the atom bomb, and goes on through unemployment, inflation, and depression; foreign policy; government controls and waste; civil liberties; conservation of natural resources; labor-management troubles; subsidized agriculture; secularized religion and lax morals; health insurance, housing, old age, education, urbanization, and industrialization. To these could be added many more— leisure, communications, pressure groups, crime, culture.

But all these problems do not stir all Americans. As problems have grown bigger and more remote, apathy has overcome so many citizens that apathy itself must be considered a major problem. From this symptom and the symptoms revealed by all the other problems, it is easy to conclude that the American System is pervaded with a mortal sickness. Many have done so. But it is still a false conclusion. For it ignores three basic facts about problems: (1) that they are inherent frictions in the growth of every society, and when one appears to be "solved" it has merely reached a stage where its new symptoms have not yet aggravated men into dealing with them; (2) that problems are interdependent, and a particular solution to a problem may become largely unnecessary when other allied problems are successfully attacked; and (3) that the deeper the problem the slower the process. Let us look at a few examples.

Few would debate the assertion that the greatest failure of American democracy has been its failure to achieve a real emancipation of the Negro. Militant agitation to free the Negro from slavery went on for forty years before it reached its climax in the Civil War; and for the next eighty years efforts to secure real as well as legal freedom and equality for the Negro made slow progress. Along with such antidemocratic practices as poll taxes, Jim Crow laws, and Ku Klux Klan terrorism, inadequate schools and racial discrimination by non-Negroes continued to deprive the Negro of his citizenship. Nevertheless, by 1940 the status of the nation's 13 million Negroes was markedly changed. Illiteracy had dropped from 81 per cent to less than 15 per cent, and nearly two-thirds of those under twenty were in school. Poll taxes had been eliminated by three Southern states, so that by 1940 the number of Negroes voting in the South rose to 211,000.

By that year also, only 34 per cent of Negro workers, formerly chained to the land in a very menial capacity, were working as farm laborers, despite the fact that three-fourths of the Negro population remained in the agricultural South.

In the last ten years the changes have come with extraordinary speed. By 1950, less than 18 per cent of all Negro workers were on farms and over half of these were farmers or farm managers. Of those who had left the farms, less than half were in domestic or other service jobs, 15 per cent were laborers, and the rest were scattered in industry (28 per cent), clerical and sales work (6 per cent), or working as proprietors or managers or in the professions (6 per cent). During the war Negroes in civilian jobs increased by more than a million, and in the last few years the drive for Negro civil rights has bowled ahead. New laws have not secured Negro rights, but they have improved the Negro's opportunities to fight for them.

Four years after the Supreme Court held "white primaries" unconstitutional, over a million Negroes in the South voted in the presidential election. Two more Southern states dropped the poll tax (leaving six to go), and a succession of local court decisions banned segregation of Negroes on golf courses, in restaurants, bars, theatres, swimming pools, public schools. The Supreme Court ruled segregation out of interstate buses and ordered state schools to furnish equal facilities to Negroes. The armed services moved to banish segregation, and a stack of state laws were passed against racial discrimination in employment, education, militias, public housing.

The advance in Negro education shows up in the enrollment of over 91,000 students in ninety-one Negro colleges (there were fifteen schools offering some college work in 1909), with nearly 3,000 more in non-Negro colleges. As illiteracy fell to 11 per cent, the American Negro population was estimated to be only about a generation behind the rest of the nation, educationally, and thus to have achieved the fastest cultural rise of any race in history.

But, as other statistics show, the Negro problem is still thorny. Since 1900 the average male Negro life expectancy has been increased by nearly twenty-six years, but there is still only one Negro doctor for every 3,500 Negroes (the national ratio is one to 750), and in one Southern state (Mississippi) the ratio is one to 18,000. Though Negroes now comprise 10 per cent of the nation's population, they have access to only 1 per cent of the hospital beds. The median Negro family income in 1948 was less than $1,800, or 47 per cent lower than the comparable white family income. Urban living on a low income has intensified Negro hardships, and those who can afford to live in better homes encounter a new, embittering "middle-class" discrimination.

In the South, segregation continues the rule in restaurants, stations, theatres, schools, barber and beauty shops. Since, paradoxically, Negroes and whites may, for example, mix freely while at work, shopping, or riding in elevators, the Southerner may argue that segregation is not discrimination but a practice rooted in "tradition." The tradition is vague but very real, and some Southerners might privately say that it was sharpened not only by the threat of Negro political power but by old lingering fears of miscegenation, disease, and vengefulness, and by subtler reactions stirred by contacts with a dark-skinned people. At any rate the tradition is not rational. It is as false to assume it is as to assume that problems can be permanently solved.

No statistics about America are more baffling than those that reveal how its citizens are aging. Fifty years ago only 4 per cent of the population was over sixty-four and two-thirds of these people were working. By last year the percentage of people in this group had nearly doubled, while the total number, 11,300,000, was about four times the 1900 figure. And less than half of these people are now in the labor force. In the same period the total of those forty-five or over has risen to 40 million, or to more than a quarter of the population, and the percentage of those at work has dropped from 88 to 75. Furthermore it is estimated that within ten years those sixty-five and over will be 18 million strong, and by 1980 half the population will be forty-five or older.

It is notable here that these changes are the result of the successful attacks that science has made on national health problems. Advances in medicine have so swiftly cut the mortality from disease that an American child born today has a life expectancy of sixty-seven years; a century ago the average American life span was only forty years. Moreover, the present life span promises to be lengthened through research on the degenerative processes of aging, since dramatic experiments with the hormones ACTH and cortisone indicate that the biological slowdown of old age can be halted and even reversed, at least temporarily. Concurrently with the lengthening of life, the long decline in the birth rate (now 24 per 1,000) has lowered the proportion of young people (eighteen and under) in the population. The net effect is a gradual aging of the "productive population," those between twenty and sixty-four who now labor and pay taxes.

These demographic facts, however, merely introduce the growing problems of security. For the "old age" group is also being expanded downward to include many of those over forty. Chiefly responsible for this are the present policies of industry and labor. Many surveys have shown that the common practice in industry is not to hire people over forty or forty-five. Among the reasons for such discrimination may be pension-plan requirements, e.g., compulsory retirement at sixty-five, length-of-service clauses, and other actuarial restrictions. Many employers also believe that older workers are less efficient, more apt to get sick or hurt, even though these beliefs have been repeatedly discredited. The seniority systems of unions further inhibit the hiring of older personnel. In any case, the man over forty who loses his job is finding it much harder to get another. To help him, some fourteen "Forty-Plus" clubs have sprung up in the U.S., and at least one state—Massachusetts—has already passed a law to restrain employers from discriminating against older workers in hiring and firing.

But laws cannot stop the inexorable increase of older people or the shrinking effect that taxes and inflation have had on pensions and social-security payments. That the demand for government old-age assistance will go up accordingly seems inevitable. Since Americans over forty-five already constitute nearly half the population of voting age, the pressure of this group could become politically irresistible. Among those alarmed by this prospect, Eric Johnston foresees "a running political warfare between youth and age in this country, age clamoring for more and more retirement benefits, youth refusing to shoulder the added costs." The costs could be astronomical. The payment of even $100-a-month government pensions to all those over sixty-five would cost some $12 billion a year today, and more than twice that by 1980. But whatever the figures were, they would still reflect only the economic problems of an aging population. And it is the other problems of age that cast the darkest shadows.

The American dream of a comfortable retirement after a life of hard work persists, but it is no longer a simple dream of ease, of going fishing, of reading, knitting, or sitting in the sun. Such pleasures may have been the goal of Americans in a rural and agricultural economy—and they may still sound pleasing to those not yet retired. But the shift to an urban, industrialized economy has made millions incapable of a vegetative retirement. Better health is partly responsible, since Americans now have more vigor and more years to live than their grandfathers had. More responsible, however, are the profound changes that industrialization has wrought in American ideas about living. Industrialization has not only raised the

standard of living; it has speeded living up and intensi-
fied the American dislike of idleness.

The belief that workers want to "grow old gracefully"
in retirement has been thoroughly exposed as a myth.
Surveys have shown that of those who retire in good
health at sixty-five, only one in twenty does so voluntarily. The main reasons are not economic; the fear of
being dependent or of living in poverty has been found
to be much less than the fear of being idle and unwanted
by society. Also, it is a medically established fact that the
forced retirement of active people accelerates their physical and mental deterioration. Most of those in retirement
appear to share the bitter realization of the woman in a
home for the aged who, when a visitor commented on her
comfortable chair, retorted, "Yes, and I am rocking my-
self to death in it."

In the frustrations of the aged, European critics of
American life find a vulnerable target. The charge that
Americans are cultural "barbarians" has certainly been
overdone; but it scores heavily among those old people
who live out their days just sitting by the radio or gazing at television. Certainly, if Americans had a richer
cultural life, old age would be less of a problem.

Yet the poignant frustrations of old age do not constitute the core of the problem of security. They are only
vivid symptoms of it, and many ways have been suggested to alleviate them; for example, the elimination of
compulsory retirement and the development of adult-
education programs of study, recreation, and arts and
crafts. Among those who have studied the problem the
common opinion is that as leisure increases, play and

self-expression" through hobbies and handcrafts will become the major objectives of American life. But is this really a definition of the goals toward which Americans are heading under their System? Has the utopia of the 1920's that envisioned "a chicken in every pot and two cars in every garage" been succeeded by a utopia of recreation and guided tours through the arts and crafts? Is this what the Founding Fathers meant by the Pursuit of Happiness? It is the question of goals that gives the problems of security and leisure their profundity.

Indeed, the conflict over goals has been ultimately responsible for the major problems facing the U.S. Thus, for example, while the drive toward goals of self-interest, of economic success, has produced the world's highest standard of living, it has also created a long train of problems—congested cities, depletion of natural resources, tariff and immigration walls, depressions. At the same time the drive toward the goal of equal opportunity has developed another succession of problems—civil rights, industrial conflict, government controls. From the conflict between these goals arises the great problem of social management in an industrial society. Great though this problem is, it is but part of a much greater one.

This overriding problem, based on philosophical principles, is to maintain the balance between the development of the individual, the environment, the techniques, and the goals. And the kernel of this great problem is the development of the potentials within the individual. No society has yet existed in which men have achieved the goal of fulfilling those potentials, and it is painfully clear that men are far from this ideal today. But there is powerful evidence to show that of all societies in recorded history, that established under the American Proposition has provided the most favorable conditions for individual growth. The essential condition is freedom—not merely the negative freedom *from* social, political, and economic restrictions, but the positive freedom *to* develop, to change, to experiment—to carry on, that is, a permanent revolution.

These two kinds of freedom are continuously conflicting. The conflict has appeared wherever some Americans wanted to change things that other Americans thought satisfactory. A century ago, for example, attempts to establish tax-supported free public schools were violently opposed by taxpayers, churches, slaveholders, politicians, teachers, and non-English-speaking groups who wanted no restrictions on their freedom to educate—or not to educate—their children as they chose. In this case the freedom to experiment with public education won out. In other cases, the freedom to change the status quo has been lost—the right of secession, for example—or, as in "the Noble Experiment" of prohibition, it has triumphed only briefly.

Whatever the outcome, the continuing American task has been to maintain both the negative and positive freedoms. As the social structure grows more complex, the task gets harder. The difficulty is not to be found in the obvious denials of freedom, such as those which lately reached their climax in "loyalty oaths" for scientists, teachers, and civil servants. Though editors, columnists, and others especially sensitive to censorship have rallied against these restrictions on freedom, they are the logical result of military demands for security, and of the public realization that the American System is at war with the Communist System. That these restrictions do not mean that American freedom from censorship is dying is evident in the steady shower of criticisms that the American press has hurled against the government for the last eighteen years. The serious losses of freedom are those not consciously recognized as such. Quite possibly these may result from the American passion for mass production, which has standardized not only material products but also those of education, communication, and entertainment. To the degree that such standardization has molded American thinking and judgment it has made conformity a habit which, consciously or unconsciously, tends to restrict the freedom to change.

The implications in such a tendency lead directly to the large questions that have been raised about the state of U.S. culture, and in their efforts to explain the source of the nation's problems, historians and sociologists have come forth with various explanations. One explanation is that the blame lies in "cultural lag," i.e., that social, political, and economic institutions have fallen too far behind the advances of science and technology. Another is that the problems of society arise from the continual conflict between realists who accept the status quo and idealists who yearn to improve it. Others describe the problems in psychological terms, a notable thesis being that of Dr. Erich Fromm, whose diagnosis is an American fear of responsibility, a desire to "escape from freedom." To many others, including scientists as well as theologians, the American dilemma is spiritual, caused by a lack of faith in God or Christianity, or the loss of moral and aesthetic values.

There is truth in all of these explanations. But the central problem revealed by them is the development of the individual. Only as the individual American matures can his society mature. And the responsibility for his development rests on no one but himself. He cannot expect to become mature by means of better government, or an improved environment, or a higher standard of living, or technological mastery. While these have made his living easier, they have not contributed directly to his psychological and spiritual maturity. Indeed, American concern for material welfare and security is generally considered to inhibit such growth. Yet the fact is that this concern has indirectly started the individual toward psychological and spiritual maturity. For it has vastly complicated the nature of his problems and thereby forced him to look harder for new solutions.

He has been encouraged in his search by the new science of psychology, the influence of which is on the rise throughout the nation. Modern psychology is changing the outlook of the individual toward many of the problems that confront him. The eighteenth century assumed, or appeared to assume, that man was primarily a rational animal. And the belief that man would naturally follow the dictates of his "reason" was accepted throughout the nineteenth century and well into the twentieth. Even today many reformers take it for granted that once men see the unreasonableness or injustice of a situation, their "reason" will move them to correct it. Sometimes it certainly does. But rationalistic optimism has been profoundly altered by Pavlov, who showed that man's reflexes were conditioned by his environment, and by Freud, who showed that man was impelled by drives and motives he might never be conscious of. As a result of these and other researches, and the marked rise in psychotherapy, the realization is growing that while man possesses the faculty of reason, he is slow to develop it and rarely allows it alone to guide him. Much of what he had *called* thinking is shown to be rationalized feeling; it is his conscious and subconscious desires and appetites, not his reason, that commonly dominate his behavior.

In the light of these discoveries it is no longer possible to make many of the assumptions about man and society that once seemed self-evident. One such is that men are incurably addicted to their own selfish ends, that human nature cannot change. Another is that men want only the security of material comfort. Still another is that men can achieve a problem-free society by solving the economic, political, and social problems facing them. These propositions and similar generalities are no longer tenable in view of what has been and is being discovered about man, the psychic being. One of the greatest contributions of modern psychology has been to make more and more people aware that the real problems lie *within* man, not in the external complexities of his world.

It is true that the inner search, whether psychological or religious, has only just begun (in modern terms) and that the signs of success are still few. But one of the most hopeful signs is the growing sense of responsibility, as described in the next chapter, that individuals in American labor and management are acquiring about social problems and relationships, particularly in their efforts to work out techniques of participation. Another sign is the awakening of American citizens to their responsibilities toward the rest of the world. The realization of such responsibilities is characteristic evidence of approaching psychological maturity. Comparable evidence of spiritual maturity has not yet appeared. The recent federation of twenty-nine Protestant and Eastern Orthodox groups in the National Council of the Churches of Christ may be a first step, but organized religion has yet to find ways to make the attainment of religious experience and insight—not simply morals and ethics—an impelling American goal. As the complex of his problems develops, the individual American may retreat into apathy; but he is more likely to reach a new perspective on his present goals. No one can say what his new goals will be. But it is the essential virtue of the American Proposition that he shall be free to gain them.

A Note on the Technological Revolution

From a certain point of view, most of the great problems of our time have arisen from the more or less violent impact of technology on the institutions and beliefs of mankind. Throughout the civilized world the technical revolution has shaken not only governments but the most elementary concepts of government. It has created the social problem, as we know it in modern terms. And while in one sense setting men free, or giving them new hope of freedom, it has in another sense threatened them with

*new forms of enslavement. One of the great achieve-
ments of the American system has been its ability to
absorb, and even to encourage, the technical revolution,
without forfeiting its own basic characteristics. Nevertheless, the action and counter-action between the two
has given rise to formidable problems. It is essential,
therefore, in facing the problems of free men, to have a
clear idea of just what the technical revolution is.*

The measure of the technological revolution, which
is not peculiarly American but belongs to the world,
is horsepower. There are other, less clumsy measures, but
none so graphic. When in 1790 James Watt set out to
sell his double-acting steam engine in rural England, he
studied the amount of work a horse could do in an hour,
multiplied it by 1⅓ for safety, got a value of 500 foot-
pounds a second, and found he could claim the equivalent of 2 horsepower for his engine without fear of
farmer reprisals. From the start Watt's term was not
closely accurate. But visibly teaming and straining behind his horsepower symbol of a machine age were the
beasts of burden which, in the long struggle up from the
caves, had been man's only mobile and exterior sources
of power in building a home on earth.

Today the contrasts are staggering in size and portent.
As recently as 1940, the proud pinnacle of electric-power
output alone in this country stood at the equivalent of
226 billion horsepower-hours a year. In the interim this
has been more than doubled to 514 billion horsepower-
hours, from an installed generating capacity of over 112
million horsepower. Add to this the 5 billion horsepower,

more or less, of automobiles and trucks on U.S. roads, and the 300 million horsepower in farm and industrial tractors, and the 120 million horsepower in railroads, and the 15,500,000 active horsepower in commercial aircraft engines. (Military aircraft horsepower is unavailable for security reasons.) Still, this does not begin to exhaust the horsepower in the U.S. It does not include direct heat energy generated in industry's stationary boilers, almost impossible to estimate, which may provide nearly as much horsepower as all other categories combined. No accurate energy census has ever been taken. Engineers, doodling on pads, only come up with startling approximations. In mechanical energy alone it works out to over 4,000 horsepower-hours per person per year in the U.S. This is about double the horsepower working for every person in the nearest industrial commonwealth, Great Britain, and about thirty-three times the horsepower-per-citizen of India or China.

But these bare and boastful figures are not important in themselves. In the crises of our times the historians have dug back deeply into sources. What is apparent at once is that this technical industrial civilization is a growth from all the past. All ages, all races, have had part in it. Even the cave man passed on his technological inventions of fire-making and stone-shaping to the agrarian age that succeeded him, as the agrarian age in turn passed on its inventions of the plow, the wheel, the ship, weaving, pottery-making, mining, metalworking, and writing.

Before Watt could invent his steam engine and England's dark, satanic mills could employ it, a vast accumulation of inventions by anonymous and less well-known inventors had to take place, as well as an accumulation of pure science and thought by a host of original thinkers from the Greeks to Roger Bacon (1214–1294) to Isaac Newton (1642–1727). The veritable explosion of eighteenth- and nineteenth-century invention, which marked a true turning point in history, was the work of no one class or nation.

For technology is simply the common hoard of man's tools and techniques, built up as inanimate but supremely human extensions of the individual, or group, to survive and understand and shape and control the elements. This pursuit has engaged the spirit of man as steadily as his religion and his art, though many will not and cannot admit it to equal status. It has had a continuity possessed by few other human activities. No scrap of man's technical hoard thus far has ever been permanently lost. While gods have changed (without changing man's basic religious impulse) and dynasties have tumbled (without changing his search for better political forms), the hoard has steadily grown, sometimes slower, sometimes faster, but never stopped. It advanced even in the Middle Ages, under an authoritarian church generally in opposition.

Technology has moved up under all past forms; it has reached a new, accelerating speed under free capitalism; and it will move up into whatever new advance may come in man's social order. But everywhere technology has moved fastest and furthest in those interstices of history between the tyrannies of church, state, and economics where men were free and channels of communication were open.

Founded in the century when free institutions and the Age of Enlightenment were all in the ascendency, at the precise moment when the great explosion of horsepower was taking place, on an open continent of vast natural resources, open to all races and creeds, and with all the heritage of Europe behind it, the U.S. unfolded the technical revolution in the climate in which it best thrives. Use of technology for the individual and the mass has here reached the highest point in history.

Hardly any of man's ancient physical slaveries remain unmechanized, from the cutting of forests or digging of ditches to clipping of suburban lawns. In such heavy developments as earth-moving machinery, backbreaking manual labor has been virtually eliminated. (Unskilled labor in 1950 dropped to 6 per cent of the U.S. working population, while semiskilled rose to 20 per cent.) On the farm, a combination of mechanization, chemistry, genetics, and agricultural science has more than doubled man-hour productivity since 1900, while the ratio of farm labor to population has dropped to the lowest point in history (one out of eighteen as against three out of four in 1800). Last year alone the output of small engines and fractional-horsepower electric motors reached 28 million units, with a total of 25 million horsepower, for every conceivable job, from digging a garden and sawing a board to beating an egg. With a still imperfect distribution, these extensions of the individual have served him more widely in the U.S. than anywhere on earth.

The U.S. has contributed many inventions to the technical store, but its greatest and most enduring contribution has been in assembling and organizing inventions to

183

mass-production ends. Eli Whitney's design of inter-changeable parts and Henry Ford's continuous assembly line, endlessly modified, set the pattern for modern world industry. While the assembly line brought the work to the worker, tending to enslave him to the rhythm of the line, a vast development of electric motors and electronic controls now bring power to the work, striking back, as free technology has always struck back, at slavery, even of its own making.

In the last decade both ends of the production line, the feeding in of materials and carrying away of product, have felt the impact of another peculiarly American innovation. An unspectacular horde of conveyer belts, fork trucks, tote cars, and pallets have made spectacular cuts in handling costs, replacing the human back with a mechanized system of materials handling moving out in all directions.

Even more spectacular and less well recognized, though it is on a par with the invention of the assembly line, is the continuous-flow chemical plant. This had its precursors in the German gas-synthesis plants of the early part of the century and in the big semi-automatic synthesis plants of Union Carbide & Carbon, du Pont, and Allied Chemical in the late twenties. But on its present scale of automatism, the continuous-flow innovation dates only from 1942, when Standard Oil Co. (N.J.) and M. W. Kellogg Co. erected the first of the oil industry's giant fluid catalytic crackers; from there the continuous-flow principle has been moving back revolutionarily into the chemical industry. In these tremendous new plants the raw material, fluid or gas, flows continuously in at one end, passes through intricate processing stages, and debouches in a twenty-four-hour stream of products at the other. The whole plant is run from central control rooms by a few men gazing at automatic-control instruments. The power of such technology to create new industries is now unsurpassed. In one direction alone it has brought into being in twenty years some 4,000 fabricators of plastic products doing a business of about $240 million last year. Chemical technology has moved so fast that this industry in all its growing ramifications accounts for about a fifth of the total national product, and in growth potential is now the premier industry of the century.

On the mechanical plane the story is the same. In transportation a vast development of pipelines, long-distance conveyer belts, and other unorthodox vehicles has demonstrated an ability to cut transportation costs 25 to 50 per cent below older forms of conveyances. And the American Ordnance Association reports that advances in production techniques of only the last five years, involving new forging methods and others under security wraps, can increase the output of bombs, rockets, artillery, small arms, and other ordnance more than ten times over the peak of World War II. That is the way technology moves.

But clearly foreshadowed in modern technology—as clearly as almost all of today's basic inventions were foreseen in the great awakening of science in the seventeenth and eighteenth centuries—is an entirely new level of controls and energy. In the new high-speed electronic calculating machines, industrial television, magnetic-tape recorders, and other components, are the means of achieving the completely automatic production or assembly line, as well as even more revolutionary automatic machines for taking over all the dull, routine tasks of business and government offices. Few minds have begun to apply themselves as yet to the problems in such upheavals.

The rise of power has had more shock effect. Already the aircraft jet engine has climbed to 15,000 horsepower in a single unit, and the liquid-fuel rocket has climbed to 750,000. Meanwhile, the potential 30 billion horsepower-hours in one ton of atomic fuel, which men are devising ways of unlocking for good or evil, raises another specter over the world.

Technology has indeed reached an entirely new level of power, another great turning point. The newness is twofold: On the one hand, the potential power level of destruction has been and is being geometrically raised, with the A bomb no longer first on the new scale, being preceded by such untried devices as radioactive dust clouds and germ warfare—all of which are as open to Russia as to us. On the other hand, the likewise increasing power, complexity, and interdependence of factors in advanced technological societies make such societies increasingly vulnerable to that destruction.

Meanwhile the disparities and unbalances of power levels in the world grow ever more pointed. Of the world's visible reserves of energy from all sources, half lie in the U.S. and Russia; another third lie in nine other countries; and the remainder are spread thinly, in concentrations nowhere reaching one per cent, over all the other nations of the globe. It behooves us who espouse

186

freedom to remember that the society that brings to this more or less impoverished half of the world the tools and fruits of modern technology will be the ultimate, beneficent, and dominant society of the earth.

INDIVIDUALISM

COMES OF AGE

IN EUROPE, especially in France, there has developed
an important political philosophy referred to as the
Third Force, whose admirable aim is to segregate out the
extremes of left and right, to create a middle-of-the-road
democracy, free of totalitarian control, whether Communist or Fascist. To this aim Americans would overwhelmingly subscribe. But the American who troubles to
inquire discovers that capitalism is classed by most members of the Third Force with the forces of the right.
European middle-of-the-roaders, in other words, are not
prepared to go along with the kind of economic system
inherent in the American way of life.

This discovery comes to the average American as a
shock. For if he has given any thought to these matters
he can hardly have escaped the conviction that the real
third force in the world is the system of political economy

that has developed in this country. Here indeed, he feels, is the middle ground on which humanity can take its stand against totalitarianism of any kind. Here is a set of principles capable of specific application in such a way as to maintain the dignity of the human being, while providing him with the abundant life. What has happened thus to separate the European Third Force from American doctrine?

The answer is twofold. In the first place there has been an almost total failure in communication. As was pointed out in Chapter IV, U.S. capitalism has been in the process of a transformation, with the result that it now bears little resemblance to the classical brand (against which, for example, Karl Marx launched his attack more than a hundred years ago). European capitalism, on the other hand, has not gone through this transformation. Consequently, when Europeans talk about capitalism, they are referring to something that no longer exists in America, something that the overwhelming majority of Americans would wish to see abolished.

Moreover, the very structure of American capitalism is different from what the dogmatists think capitalism is. We have in America what Whitney Griswold, President of Yale University, has called a "mixed state." Ownership is predominantly private, but it is not exclusively so; and even private ownership has in many instances been highly "socialized." At one end of the scale you find such a business as metal scrap, which still operates on a dog-eat-dog basis, the way old-fashioned capitalism was supposed to. At the other end you find such a thing as the government-owned-and-managed Tennessee Valley Authority. In between are all shades of the economic rainbow: government "regulation," as of the railroads; industries like the garment industry, where well-integrated unions not only set wages and working conditions but provide in many ways for the security and happiness of their members; powerful and efficient producer cooperatives; and many big corporations, some unionized, some not, that have undertaken comprehensive social programs of their own.

The first answer to the above question, then, is that Americans have somehow failed to make clear to the world what modern American capitalism is like, with the result that the critics of American capitalism are criticizing something that almost literally does not exist. That basic failure in communication is discussed at greater length in the next chapter, "Have We Any Friends?" There is, however, a second aspect to the question, which underlies the first: Americans themselves have not yet awakened to the full implications, in modern terms, of their own system. They are aware that they have something; but unlike the founders of their own country, they have been unable to give expression to basic truths they have discovered. For the fact is that there exist in America today the makings of a new doctrine, a new answer to totalitarianism, whether of the left or right; an answer rooted in the universals of the American Proposition (as all valid American answers must be), but capable of transformation to meet the needs and aspirations of other peoples dedicated to freedom.

As pointed out in Chapter III, "The American System," the key word in the development of the U.S. has been "Liberty." This word meant the emancipation of the individual; he was to be set free *by law* to "pursue happiness" according to his own definitions, including the free exercise of the right of private property. Economically this experiment was a huge success. It resulted in a vast industrial development and a fabulous rise in the standard of living for everyone.

The very success of the experiment, however, created a new kind of problem, which we today call the "social" problem. This problem originates in the now all-too-familiar fact that the rewards of the industrial system, where it is left to its own devices, are unfairly and uncertainly distributed. Workers who are dependent upon that system for their livelihood are threatened with a new form of slavery—slavery to the machine. Their standard of living may be pushed downward, relatively speaking. And they are at the same time exposed to the violent swings of the economic cycle, which may deprive them of their ability to earn a living at all.

These familiar truths have resulted in the development of the thesis that it is socially undesirable to leave the management of an industrial system in private hands. For private management, pursued for the purpose of private gain, it is maintained, can take into account only the profits of the owners, not the needs of the workers or of the community. In order to provide for those needs— so runs the thesis—it is necessary to turn over to the state full powers of regulation, of control, of general economic management—indeed, the actual ownership of the facilities. The state will then—so the socialists tell us—replace the selfish decisions of private parties with rational decisions for the good of all.

Whatever flaws there may be in this argument, no industrial country in the world has been able altogether to resist it. Even in the U.S., where resistance has been greatest, there has been a tremendous increase in the power of government over economic affairs. Nevertheless, resistance in the U.S. has been very great; and there are those who believe that nothing less is involved in the debate than the American Proposition itself. The argument for social management by the state is based upon the assumption that private parties are, of necessity, socially irresponsible. The Proposition, on the other hand, is based upon the contrary assumption of individual, of *private*, responsibility. Virtually all of the founders were explicit on this point; they were aware that their great system of Liberty could not work unless human beings were fit to meet and discharge the responsibilities of Liberty. It is hard to see, therefore, how the founders could have escaped the admission that the "social" problem constitutes a fundamental test of the Proposition. If private parties are indeed socially irresponsible, then government responsibility *must* replace private responsibility in the social field; and this, as is now abundantly apparent, means the almost indefinite extension of government power over private lives.

What we have as yet failed to understand, however, is that the Proposition itself meets the social problem head on. Naturally the founders made no pronouncements about "social responsibility" as such, because the problem

192

as we know it did not exist in their day. Yet the genius of the fundamental thinking that brought America into being does not lie in its literal but in its intuitive character, as has been demonstrated time after time with the Constitution itself; and an intuitive treatment of the Proposition, as set forth in the Declaration of Independence, reveals hitherto unsuspected possibilities. It can result, indeed, in a transformation that provides the groundwork for a solution to the social problem of our time.

An elucidation of this transformation was attempted in a recent article in FORTUNE entitled "The Greatest Opportunity on Earth." There it was pointed out that the three basic Rights of the Proposition—Life, Liberty, and the Pursuit of Happiness—represent "three different spheres of life," each involving a different *kind* of right. The Right to Liberty was called the *political* Right, because it has to do primarily with the political safeguards (*i.e.*, the civil liberties) that protect the emancipated individual. The Right to the Pursuit of Happiness, on the other hand, involves us in not merely political but cultural and spiritual matters. What it means, in brief, "is that the individual is guaranteed an opportunity to fulfill himself as he may choose . . . It is a fundamental guarantee to the human spirit, an appeal to freedom, not only within the law but beyond the law, in the realm of human aspiration."

Yet the Proposition, it was pointed out, has to do with even a third *kind* of right, summarized under the heading of the Right to Life. This is neither political, on the one hand, nor spiritual, on the other. The threat to life may be a question merely of violence, but in modern industrialized society it goes far beyond this. The threat has "become economic. In an industrial city like Pittsburgh, for example, it is sheer hypocrisy to talk about the Rights of Man in terms only of Liberty and the Pursuit of Happiness. Since meat, milk, and vegetables will not grow on Pittsburgh's streets, when a worker loses his job he cannot eat—that is, he cannot live. If the American Proposition is to have any meaning in Pittsburgh, therefore, an *economic* Right must be established. And this is none other than the eighteenth-century Right to Life." While this interpretation of the Proposition might stir up considerable scholarly debate, it nevertheless has the virtue of driving straight to the heart of the question. In its light the whole social struggle of our time is seen to center around the Right to Life. Indeed, this is precisely the meaning of state socialism. People have turned to the state, not because they have foregone the Right to Life, but on the contrary because they insist upon its primacy. It is the *first* Right, the implementation of which is **more** important, even, than the Right to Liberty. The interpretation thus verifies the amazing intuition of the American founders.

Yet if this interpretation is accepted, then the whole social question hinges upon a question of fact. *Is the assumption valid, that private parties are of necessity socially irresponsible?* If it is, then the Proposition must be so extensively modified, to provide for governmental responsibility, that there can be good question of its usefulness. If, on the other hand, the assumption is invalid,

194

then Americans should awaken to the new challenge that was defined in "The Greatest Opportunity on Earth."

Now the assumption in question was first officially made in the U.S. by Franklin Roosevelt's New Deal and has been preserved and carried further by the Fair Deal under Harry Truman. And there can be no question of its validity *up to a certain point.* That is to say, up to 1933, when the New Deal first made the assumption, too many private parties in the U.S. had indeed conducted themselves in a socially irresponsible manner. But on the other hand, it must also be said that there exists no proof whatever that private parties are incapable of responsible social thought and action. On the contrary, the burden of the evidence is all the other way. There is evidence on every hand that the American people, including American businessmen, are even anxious to assume responsibilities for the implementation of the Right to Life: thus to derive, from the Proposition itself, a new and dynamic solution for the social problem.

The attitude in question could scarcely be better illustrated than by the remark that the president of one of the biggest steel corporations recently made to a group of friends who had gathered to hear about his development plans. "The first question we have to decide," he said, "is what capacity for the steel industry would best serve the interests of society as a whole." It was a quiet remark, and neither the speaker nor his listeners paid any particular attention to it. That fact, perhaps, is a measure of the social progress American capitalism has been making.

The corporation in question is not the biggest in the industry; and even if it were, its decisions could not, of course, determine the question of the industry's total capacity, the way a government bureau could. The social planner, therefore, would object that it is in fact impossible for private parties to do effective planning. Yet this objection overlooks a number of important factors at work in any business situation. Plans made by one company become known to others. The reasoning behind them also becomes known: if it is sound, it has great influence; if unsound, few follow suit. "Collusion" is forbidden by the antitrust laws, but the follow-the-leader principle works with great effect because nobody wants to be left out. "Private planning" of this kind is, of course, slower than state planning; but it has the great advantage of mitigating the possibility of serious error. If the state planner is wrong, the error is total, because it has been inflicted on all concerned. In private planning there is almost always one or several who won't go along: and he or they may turn out to be right.

The history of employee pensions in America provides a perfect example of how "private planning" works. Up to 1940 only a relative handful of companies gave old-age pensions to their retiring employees. During the war many companies discovered that the tax law enabled them to provide pensions very cheaply, and there was accordingly a great increase in the number of pension plans, which reached about 7,000 by the end of 1945. But what really touched off the pension landslide was the agreement between the United Automobile Workers and Ford in 1949. The contract won by the union in that negotiation provided for pensions for all Ford hourly employees and entailed upon the company the obligation to set up a mammoth pension fund estimated at $200 million. But this was not by any means the major result. Every important union in the country began to demand pensions, and every wide-awake corporation of any size recognized the justice—or at least the inevitability—of the demand. As a result, in little more than a year old-age pensions have virtually become standard practice in American mass-production industry. It would be wrong to say that all American businessmen have become social angels. Many of them have bucked the trend hard, some are still bucking it. Nevertheless, every year more businessmen see the light and some few even become "missionaries." The result is that American business is erecting a social structure that many a state planner would envy. The American worker, of course, has won that most basic of social rights, the right to organize and bargain collectively. And this in turn has brought about a very rapid transformation. The wage level has advanced faster than corporation dividends, for example. In addition, as already pointed out in Chapter IV, many contracts include valuable (and costly) fringe benefits. Some call for compulsory arbitration of industrial disputes, others contain various clauses regarding job maintenance, to increase the worker's security.

But the benefits, the profit-sharing systems, the incentive plans, and so forth, are not really the point. The important thing is the underlying attitude. The American businessman is by no means prepared to admit the worker as a literal partner, but he is increasingly aware that if

197

the enterprise system is to persist, a *kind* of partnership must be created. It is proper for an enterprise to risk dollars. It is not proper—most businessmen will admit—for a dollar-making venture to risk human lives, health, or the basic security of those who work for it. And those who see the problem most clearly carry this attitude even further. The remarkable Scanlon plan, touched on in Chapter IV, is an effort to work out a true and realistic partnership between owners and workers. Such participation opens the way to the evolution of a true industrial democracy, wholly in line with American traditions—and wholly beyond the capacity of state planners to achieve.

The Right to Life, therefore, is being implemented in America by *private* means in two important ways: (1) by industrial planning with the general welfare of society in mind, and (2) by radical improvements in industrial relations. Yet if this were the whole story, it would not need telling here. What makes the current American development exciting from a social-planning standpoint is the eagerness of all Americans to step in and carry out social tasks wherever the opportunity presents itself. In 1947 a Gallup poll revealed that there were more than 50 million people in the U.S. who would be willing to serve without pay on committees of private citizens to study community problems such as housing, strikes, health, juvenile delinquency, unemployment, and education. Seven out of ten of the leading men of the nation, Gallup reported, said they would be willing to take time to help solve such problems. The reader can verify this finding by turning to Chapter VII. Most of the myriad activities described in that chapter are social activities; many are activities which, in socialistic lands, are the direct responsibility of the state; some are as farsighted as social planners could hope to be; still others, such as Alcoholics Anonymous, perform a *creative* social function wholly beyond the grasp of the state, having within them the power actually to change the society. Yet these activities are all voluntary.

In this new way of thinking, solutions will differ in different communities. In most communities, for example, the fire department is publicly owned and operated; but in many small communities fire-fighting is still in the hands of volunteer fire brigades. Easton, Connecticut, has a community ambulance, privately supported and free to all. What is the use of being doctrinaire about these things? The point is to get something done that needs to be done for the benefit of all concerned. Maybe the government has to do it; but in eight or nine cases out of ten you don't have to wait for government at all— you can get it done right at the community level in your own way.

Indeed, anyone interested in this approach will find in the U.S.A. an enormous reservoir of human energy available for the purpose of voluntary social action and management. The number of examples that might be cited reaches into the thousands. In Alexandria, Indiana, for instance (population 6,000), the streets were in terrible repair, but the contractors estimated the cost of fixing them at $60,000, and this sum could not be met by the town budget. The citizens therefore organized a "paving bee," bought $3,000 worth of asphalt and patching material, and did the job themselves. In Bat Cave, North Carolina (population 175), the citizens have built themselves a hospital on the same mutual basis. In Ratcliff, Texas (population 200), which could not afford a full-fledged hospital, they banded together to provide emergency services. And so forth and so on across the nation. The Twentieth Century Fund and N.B.C. have devoted a whole radio series to this kind of thing, called *The People Act*.

An elaboration of such examples could scarcely make the principle clearer. *The basis of American economic development has been private initiative in economic matters; the basis of American social development must be private initiative in social matters.* The only difference is that whereas everyone recognizes the former principle, the latter has been generally overlooked—lost, in fact, in a jumble of "ideological" arguments. Indeed, one who seriously investigates the evidence must stand aghast at the assumption that has hung like a cloud over the domestic economy for the past seventeen years—that private parties in America are of necessity socially irresponsible. The mounting evidence documents precisely the opposite thesis: that the American people are hungry for social action, not at the governmental, but at the voluntary community level.

The key that will unlock these unused social forces is a new type of social legislation. During the last seventeen years almost all such legislation has been designed to vest in *government* the initiative for social action. This has had its obvious advantages for the administration in power, which can claim credit for the initiative so vested; in 1949 Truman's State of the Union message referred to "opportunities" for government no less than eleven times. But in the long run "opportunities for government" can only lead Americans down the blind alley of state socialism. What is needed, in effect, is a new government attitude; an attitude wholly in conformance with the American tradition, that government exists, not for its own aggrandizement, but to protect the people's rights and to encourage *their* initiative. Out of such an attitude, applied to the social field, there would grow the type of legislation needed, designed to provide local and individual incentives for coherent social action. Such incentives, incidentally, need not be purely monetary.

In one notable instance such legislation has already been framed. In 1949 the present administration sponsored a national health plan to provide compulsory health insurance for most of the nation. The proposed act differed in technical details from the British National Insurance, but resembled it in that contributions were to be compulsory and that the national government was given enormous administrative powers. A group of progressive Republicans in the Congress, however, decided to pioneer along the lines suggested in this chapter. They framed a bill encouraging private parties to set up local medical-insurance funds, administered at the community level, but conforming to certain federal standards. They would be basically self-supporting, but federal funds would be provided according to a certain scale to enable them to reach the lowest income groups. This bill, sidetracked by the present international emergency, is still pending.

Innumerable opportunities exist for the encouragement by federal and state governments of self-help projects of this kind. All that is needed is legislation designed to implement them. For example, experiments have shown the value of self-help in solving the housing problem; Americans are handy with tools and they can build their own houses if only the capital and the necessary planning are made available. In Fayette County, Pennsylvania, a group of Quakers persuaded U.S. Steel to put up $150,000 and the Grant Foundation $60,000 for the purchase of a 200-acre farm; fifty miners then built their own houses and are now paying back the loans at the rate of $13 a month (which includes all charges). In Philadelphia the Friends have arranged financing for the reconstruction of a big northside slum on a partial self-help basis. Along another line the suggestion has been made that private citizens be encouraged to set up quasi-public community councils, primarily for the maintenance of economic security by community methods not available to a vast federal administration. Such councils might develop special work programs for the aged, giving them opportunities to defer their retirement (to the mutual advantage of the aged and the taxpayers). They could also operate community employment services to eliminate seasonal swings.

At the present time, of course, this kind of activity is more or less random in nature; it arises only where some community is lucky enough to have forceful and imaginative civic leaders. If it is to be adopted more generally, incentives must be devised. There is a danger in having the incentives come from government, because govern-

202

ment "aid" is apt to bring with it a host of government "experts" and social workers, who usually succeed in raising costs. It is preferable in most cases to have the "aid," if any, come from the state government, which is apt to be less ambitiously supplied with helpers; and this is in fact being done on a considerable scale in many states, especially under Governor Dewey in New York. However, in many cases, such as that of national health insurance, federal support is indispensable. In others, where financing is difficult, federal aid might be accepted in the form of loans to be paid back by the self-help projects.

There is still one more social area that private parties are trying to do something about. This has to do with the business cycle. The question here, however, is not the elimination of the cycle. To begin with, it is extremely doubtful whether it *can* be eliminated, even by the most rigid form of state socialism. But leaving that debate aside, it is certain that it ought not to be eliminated; even British socialists are now beginning to realize that it is essential to economic progress. The problem of the cycle is one of mitigation; adequate protection must be provided for those who are unavoidably hurt and cannot help themselves; and means must be found to anticipate and level off the swings.

It is now almost universally accepted that the first task belongs essentially to government, and that in the event of a serious depression government must also undertake very large countercyclical spending programs. But what has not been so generally realized is that private industry itself, while incapable of stemming the tide of a full depression, has been developing techniques that can have substantial stabilizing effects. These techniques involve the projection of known data into the future, for the purpose of establishing trends, which in turn form a basis for *private planning*. Every business, of course, has always had to "plan"; superficially, there is nothing new in this development, and if the question is put to the average businessman he will just dismiss it as "good management." Nevertheless, private planning is on the increase; it may well have mitigated the downswing of 1948–49, and it will almost certainly have significant effects in any future downswing. Where a fundamental trend (e.g., population) has been upward, and a company has laid plans to take advantage of it, a factor of resistance has been created that did not exist in the seat-of-the-pants kind of economy that preceded (say) World War I. The company might find it necessary, in the event of a downswing, to modify its plan; but it would probably find it unnecessary—perhaps even impossible—to cancel it altogether.

Positive stabilizing factors of this kind have been created chiefly in three fields—research, employment stabilization, and maintenance. Yet government has on the whole failed to grasp the significance of what is going on. The present revenue act inhibits "private planning" in many ways, for example, instead of encouraging it as it should. Here again, a new kind of legislation is needed. The American way of life contains the seeds of a social solution that social dogmatists have overlooked. The people are ready. Even business is ready. The problem is to exact from government an attitude at least as advanced as the "governed" already possess.

Americans are fond of saying that the state exists for the individual, not the individual for the state. Despite its truistic character, this aphorism has enormous meaning. A proletarian approach, which subordinates the individual to the group or class, represents for the American, not an advance, but a reaction—a withdrawal from the challenge of the permanent revolution. This is true even of those groups that have been most directly exposed to proletarian propaganda. And the American would add, that if a really dynamic third force is to be created, in Europe or anywhere else, the principle of individualism must constitute its foundation.

In our time individualism has clashed with the whole industrial development, mass production, and the division of labor. The key to industrialization is not independence but interdependence; no individual is self-sufficient; each is involved with countless others in complicated relationships. Dominating all this is the modern corporation, an organization of vast powers, which exacts of its managers purely impersonal decisions. It is little wonder that men have turned to the state to protect themselves in such a world.

According to the American Proposition, however, this turning to the state can only further compromise the status of the individual, who is already half lost amid forces and organizations that are too big for him. On this point the Proposition is crystal-clear: *the solution is to be found, not through a growth in government, but through a growth in the stature of the individual.* The crucial American question has always been: is the individual big enough for the responsibilities of freedom? The founders guessed "yes"—not without misgivings. But as we have seen, their guess applied principally to the question of the Right to Liberty, the political Right, which was the first that Americans developed. We are now faced with a similar development in the Right to Life—a similar problem in responsibility, though in a different field. The guess must be taken all over again, as to whether the individual is big enough to implement the Right to Life.

The concept that appears to be emerging, as the answer of the modern individual to this challenge, is the concept of the *team*. It is an old concept but it is being put to new uses. As a member of a team an individual can find full opportunity for self-expression and still retain a dynamic relationship to other individuals and to their common assignment. The concept, of course, can be gutted by bad management—and has been, on certain high-speed production lines. But where it is applied with respect for the individuals that compose the team, it constitutes a new social technique of enormous power for all concerned. This has been shown by the Hawthorne experiments and actually verified by the Scanlon "participation" system already mentioned.

For the concept of the team has the power to challenge the individual to seek his self-expression, not along purely egotistic channels, but in dynamic relationship to others, that is to say, mutually. A community is created, and through it the individual finds a higher expression of himself. A measure of giving is added to the measure of gaining. And freedom thus becomes defined in terms that cannot be referred either to laws or to dollars.

It may be that the American individual, the community to which he belongs, and the corporation into which his life is geared will fail to meet this new challenge. It may be that the forces of industrialization have carried so far, and the thinking of our leadership has been so pale, that the revolution will find its end in the shabby alleys of the mill towns, which could have been transformed into boulevards had individualism come of age. Like the founders we can only presume—and take the risk. Like them, with whatever hesitations, we must challenge the individual to grow.

HAVE WE ANY FRIENDS?

I F Americans can indeed find the means of imple-
menting the Right to Life on the basis, primarily,
of private initiative; if they can learn how to harness the
energies of individual citizens all over the land for the
solution to the social problems that so trouble the modern world, they will have made an enormous contribution to the evolution of freedom. Yet there is an axiom of
American life that may not be disregarded without dire
consequences: Americans cannot successfully achieve
their goals in a nationalistic vacuum. This axiom is inherent to the Proposition itself, which, as we have so
often stressed, is constructed of universal principles that
are held to be common to all mankind. And in a purely
pragmatic sense, it is not conceivable that a free society
in America could long endure, unless it were matched by
its own kind, whether partners or competitors, elsewhere
throughout the world.

In other words, no matter how much progress may be
made in solving domestic problems, the maintenance of

freedom here is always intimately linked with problems and goals in the field of foreign relations. And this is not only a matter of foreign *policy*, as reviewed in the next chapter. It raises a relatively new but wholly critical problem in international understanding—that is to say, a problem of communications. It is not possible to achieve an orderly evolution of freedom unless the free peoples of the world know and understand what each is trying to do. In an atmosphere of understanding new ideas will flourish, and will be tested out in various ways, so that the most useful and best may survive. Where such under-standing is lacking, however, new ideas are misunder-stood; and may even be converted, through popular mis-conceptions, into monstrosities that appear to threaten those very ideas of freedom that they were designed to serve.

Such misunderstanding exists today on a frightening scale. It exists not only between Americans and Asiatics, where the natural differences that separate eastern and western viewpoints might be expected to bring it about. It exists, most unfortunately, and perhaps most danger-ously, between America and the free world of Europe. For in Europe there has grown up a kind of myth about America, and it might one day be written that the free world destroyed itself because of it. It would not be the Big Lie of the Russians; only the fools believed that. It would be something much more inexplicable: the myth that for all our bathtubs and our cars and our skyscrapers we are without moral purpose; that we are the New Carthage—all money, no spirit; that we are, in short, a country without a soul.

If America does not destroy this myth, it will destroy America. For already it has sapped the will of our allies, made those who benefited from the ECA cynical of its purpose; and each month it grows more in virulence, ready to attack at each crisis. But even more terrible has been the effect on America herself. For when we hear the myth played back to us, we grow petulant and dismayed, and in our anger many of us can think of nothing but to pull down the pillars of a world that does not understand.

Yet the West is desperately eager to listen. That it tragically misunderstands us is not easily explained by the accusations that come so readily to American minds. Nor is it simply a matter of slicker gimmicks or extra kilowatts or more pamphlets. The failure is not technical: it is national. We have sold the world many things—sold them so well that half Europe would pack up and come over here if it could. But we have left unsold the ideas that would destroy the myth.

We talk of "A Campaign of Truth." This, certainly, is in order. But what is "the truth"? Speeches? Statistics? A day in the life of a Wisconsin farmer? Our congenital dislike of abstract thought has at last come home to roost. *We have failed to determine what it is we wish to communicate.* Once we knew very well what we were and what we wanted to be, and we thought it out into some of the most contagious prose of all time. But we went on to become the great pragmatists, so eager to be on with the job, so impatient of theory and reflection, that we worked ourselves into a moral isolationism. Why analyze America? It worked, didn't it?

Curiously, by keeping our philosophy so tacit, we have

managed to show ourselves to the world as little different from the Marxists—seeming, like them, to believe that material prosperity is an end that in itself will bring all the other qualities. Instinctively we know better, but we have never bothered to articulate for ourselves what we take for granted, much less convey it to others. And so we have talked of the manifestations of our success rather than the causes. Not for us wooly-headed theories or impractical idealism; instead, down-to-earth, hard-rock facts: the miles of cement, the telephones, the cars laid end to end—all the things, in short, our friends have envied and our enemies have conceded.

But what made the telephones and the cars possible? When we have tried to explain, it has been in a lazy man's shorthand that has obscured our national character rather than illuminated it. Thus have we prated of "individualism," when we have achieved the most horizontal, cooperative of all societies; of "competition" and "incentive economy," when we have achieved the kind of security that socialists everywhere hunger for. And we wonder why the audience is confused.

And not only have we failed to define *what* we are to say; we have failed to define *why* we want to say it. Of all the many aims of our propaganda, which is to be primary? Interestingly, almost every private organization that has thought of an overseas propaganda program of its own has stumbled on precisely this question. More to the point, so has the government.

What is the aim? Friendship? To many Americans this is the end-all. And nothing has done us more grievous harm—for we are offended terribly when love is not forth-

211

coming from others. It is quite impossible anyway. We have only to look at India; since their departure, the British, who never gave a damn whether anyone liked them or not, have become increasingly popular, while we, who did our best to expedite that departure, are becoming increasingly unpopular. The fruits of leadership do not necessarily include love, and we would do well to take the fact in our stride.

To Americanize people? No one ever puts it quite this baldly, but there lurks deep in some American breasts the feeling that there is a mystically beneficent quality in certain of our folkways, and that if only they could be exported, the chasm in understanding would be bridged. But in following this line we are indulging in a failure to isolate the particulars from the principles. After all, what was so Japanese as baseball?

To refute Communist lies? Obviously, this is an important part of any propaganda program, but as the primary aim it is a defensive course that would foredoom us to a constant shellacking. They will always be a lie ahead. Furthermore, we must recognize that anti-Communism does not fill vacuums, nor is it necessarily pro-U.S.; indeed, our biggest problem lies in those people who think we are *as bad as* the Russians.

To enlist support for American foreign policy? This is generally considered the primary aim of our propaganda effort. Spelled out, it means stressing the mutuality of each country's interests with ours; thus have we pushed ECA, North Atlantic Pact aid, the idea of national freedom, survival of the West. Is it enough? These policies are so demonstrably in the common interest that by all standards of logic they should be galvanic. Yet they are not, and the very people the policies benefit view them with mistrust. Why do they? The fact that we must ask ourselves this question helps answer the other.

Clearly, something more dynamic is needed. It is too late for mere information. If we wish our Proposition to survive we must now not only describe the revolution we began, we must extend it. And it is the Europeans themselves, as we shall see, who make the point.

The obstacles to success may seem appalling. For even when we have articulated our philosophy we have the task of projecting it over the tremendous gap in attitudes and environment that separates us from other people. And it is a gap, unfortunately, that we do not readily appreciate. We have been so unaware of basic differences that we have persisted in talking to the Europeans in terms for which there is no foreign equivalent: *participation, community relations, incentive, public relations, productivity, man-in-the-street, public opinion*—the very listing itself produces a syllabus of the American philosophy. And a glossary of misunderstanding. Taking the evocative power of these words for granted, we have assumed that "hard facts" will do the job—and that, in a sort of question-and-answer fashion, we can use prepackaged nuggets of truth to beat down each fallacy we come across. It won't work. Like the hydra, the myth is proof against piecemeal attack. *Americans are barbarians. The U.S. is a dehumanizing technocracy.* Here are the two chief elements in the myth—yet both are so

213

mutually supporting that to refute either we must trace them back to their common source.

Europe today presents an odd paradox. While "neutralism" has been reduced politically—in the words of one observer—to a "hard core of jerks," emotionally it has never been more powerful. Its underpinnings go something like this: since there is no spiritual base to the U.S., it is as culturally barren as the U.S.S.R.; its people are barbarians, and any who must accept succor from them should hate themselves for it. The thesis, of course, is put much better than this. Essayists have a whole new lexicon of psychiatric and anthropological terms for the job, and they have been using it with increasing frequency to demonstrate that the jukebox, the milk shake, or some such thing is the universal clue to America's "infantilism," "reverted uncle complex," *"Kino-Weltschmerz,"* etc.

The frightening thing is that it is the top intellectuals— the cream of Europe's professional class—who have convinced themselves most deeply. The bulk hate and fear Russia, yet the myth has so distorted their vision that, as one Frenchman has pointed out, what non-Communists seem to be fighting most is anti-Communism. And this attitude, unfortunately, cannot be shrugged off as the affectation of a small coterie. The intellectual in Europe still retains a much more commanding position in society than his American counterpart. And though he has abdicated many of the responsibilities of his leadership, every poll and survey indicates that, if nothing else, he has been saying what the majority of his countrymen feel.

Why do they think us barbarians? First, because we

214

paint ourselves as such. Few nations have put their worst foot so far forward; by our asinine emphasis on the material goodies, we have seemed, by implication, to deny the existence of anything else in American life worth bragging about. Even during the most desperate days of the war we got our message of hope so tangled up with refrigerators and cars that, as one OWI worker put it, we could have billed it as "The War That Refreshes." The commercial projection of America has gone a step further; while our information people spend millions trying to demonstrate that we are really cultural after all, the biggest information agency in the world, Hollywood, has been exporting films that seem to demonstrate the opposite—so persuasively, it might be noted, that in Austria the Russians have been saving their breath by letting several of our gangster films quietly circulate in their occupation zone.

In their own way our intellectuals have joined in the chorus. How is the world to believe that there is any spiritual content in American life, the European asks, when American higher literature is so full of despair? In part, of course, the indictment is a misreading. Certainly America's literature is a long way from Whitman's ideal to "report all heroism from the American viewpoint." Yet it is not quite so far as Europeans think, for they lack the context to see much of it for what it is—a self-criticism, a searching for values that in itself indicates a good bit of spiritual vitality in American life.

An appalling amount of our higher criticism, however, is a vituperation almost psychopathic in its intensity. "The emptiness of our American life" . . . "bourgeois in-

dustrialism" . . . "The Grand Canyon of the Big Money"
. . . "the dull horror of our lives." So goes the familiar
litany. In part it is merely verbal revenge on a social
structure that does not pay obeisance to the intellectual,
and the European can sense it as such. What he does not
realize, however, is that many of the critics have remained so unaware of the profound changes that have
taken place in our society that they are still addressing
themselves to the twenties—occasionally the 1890's.

But influential as our own self-criticisms may be, it
would be a mistake to assign them a preponderant share
in the formation of the myth. The myth reflects quite as
much about the audience as about the U.S. it is supposed
to describe—and the fact, for example, that *Rage de Vivre*
(originally, *Really the Blues*—all about marijuana, hot
jazz, etc.) is currently a best-seller in Paris demonstrates
nothing so much as the extraordinary affinity Europeans
have developed for such stuff. Furthermore, their attitude has now attained such a high degree of what the
psychologists would call "structurization" that if we
didn't supply them with the material they would probably make it up themselves. As indeed they have; two
Frenchmen, for example, have been making quite a good
thing of turning out novels of Stateside sadism and per-
version as "translations from the American." The myth
has become self-perpetuating.

Here we see the folly of assuming mere information to
be the cure for misinformation. The myth *satisfies*. In it
the intellectuals find the rationalization for their own
spiritual vacuum. For bewail as they may Europe's en-
trapment between *"les deux colosses,"* they have been

unable themselves to come up with a valid alternative. Why? They look away from themselves to chewing gum, bathtubs, and Coca-Cola for the answer.

Aesthetically, the impact of America's culture gives them a point—even the American must feel queasy when he sees a Grand Canal plastered with Coca-Cola signs. But this is not their main complaint. "What the French criticize," says *Le Monde*, after a swack at Coca-Cola, "is not so much Coca-Cola as its orchestration, less the drink itself than the civilization of which it is a mark and the symbol." *Le Monde* goes on to bemoan Buicks, Chryslers, nylon stockings, and chewing gum. "As soon as they appear these habits become an invasion. It is a question of the entire French moral landscape!" Throughout Europe intellectuals throw up their hands in the same fashion; a culture based on such wealth, goes the theme, cannot help but be contaminating.

But is even this the nub—this question of whether material riches can be reconciled with spiritual force? No; Florence, Rome, and Athens answered this one in the affirmative long ago. There is something else, more subtle, in the intellectual's animus, and it runs deep in current essays on U.S. culture. Why, the question keeps obtruding, is it so contagious? As he writes his farewells to happier days—the days when taste was still "undemocratized" and peasant girls were plump and didn't shave their legs —he writes his answer. It is a *popular* culture.

For here lies the true contagion of American culture. Whatever its aesthetics, it is above all else a proclamation to the world of the cultural enfranchisement of the

217

common man. It is *his* culture, his own version of the pursuit of happiness—and a raucous ultimatum to a society that never allowed him to trespass quite so far. But to a Europe that is still culturally an aristocracy, the symbols of his enfranchisement are often vulgar and shoddy. Is it the vulgarity of these symbols or their implicit revolutionary promise that makes them so profoundly disturbing? It is the Europeans, let us remember, not ourselves, who are obsessed by the bathtub.

Why is American culture barbarous? Europeans have an easy answer: it is the product of a *business* civilization. Thus we come to the second great element in the mythology. For the European does not see the rapidly changing, socially conscious capitalism of 1950: he sees Wall Street, Mammon—and he trembles aloud over all the false dilemmas it would imply for Europe.

Thus, it is written, America's technological triumphs pose for Europe nothing less than the issue of man versus machine. Again we are back to the old spiritual theme. True, Europe wants America's mass-production techniques—but it is haunted by the fear that in adopting them it is making a compact with the devil. To many, American technology means the dehumanization of man —Charlie Chaplin poised in the gears is still a vivid symbol—and a Europe still deep in the old craft tradition is only now beginning to grasp the compatibility of mass production with quality and humanity. Somehow we have failed badly to show that, far from being narcotized by the machine, we have been invigorated by it.

But this failure in turn stems from a greater one: our failure to demonstrate the tremendous difference between our capitalism and the capitalism of Europe. In this respect it is startling to listen to an American businessman just returned from Europe; almost invariably he will so revile its low-wage, high-markup, monopoly economics that he sounds much more the howling revolutionist than the European socialists who so mistrust him. His philosophy, however, remains uncommunicated. Not only are European capitalists utterly unconvinced of its value; the European masses are ignorant of its existence.

This double failure has had a deep effect on our relations with Europe. Translated by unregenerate European capitalism, ECA "productivity" has too often meant few benefits for the worker, but such profits for management that in Italy alone it has been hazarded that per capita there are more one-million-dollar-a-year men—paying less taxes—than there are in the U.S. To a dangerous degree, our efforts have appeared to the European worker simply a collusion between reactionary blackguards; he still can conceive of American capitalism only in terms of his own—and he is sick of it. It is high time the American businessman realized that it is not European socialism but European capitalism that is the chief block to "free enterprise." "The problem of Europe," as one observer puts it, "comes down to who is to liquidate the capitalists of Europe: the Russians—or the Americans."

These several points are best illustrated by the actual utterances of non-Communist Europeans. Here is a list of horrors culled from newspapers, periodicals, books, and radio:

"It is not what separates the United States and the Soviet Union that should frighten us, but what they have in common . . . Those two technocracies that think themselves antagonists are dragging humanity in the same direction of dehumanization . . . man is treated as a means and no longer as an end—this is the indispensable condition of the two cultures that face each other." FRANCOIS MAURIAC, Catholic anti-Communist, in *Le Figaro*.

"Americans appear the true successors of the Germans. America differs from Europe and resembles Russia, adorer of the technical." ANDRE SIEGFRIED, Protestant anti-Communist, in *Le Figaro*.

"In all the homilies to which I listened, the word *God* did not reverberate more often than the word *money* . . . It is perhaps because too often they have emptied European religions of their intellectual content that they have no choice except between music and convulsions." GEORGES FRADIER; *Esprit*.

"Of even the beginnings of the minutest embryo of a homogeneous culture there was no sign . . . A general preoccupation with trivia—I mean Coke machines, launderettes . . . laxatives and baseball—I construed as the American attempt to exclude the bigger reality . . ." ROBERT ROBINSON; the *Isis* (Oxford University).

"Why they should not be originally creative is puzzling. It is possible that the lack of the organic sense, the conviction that man is a machine . . . turns them into technicians and cuts them off from the chaos, the accidents and institutions of the creative process." V. S. PRITCHETT; *The New Statesman and Nation*.

"They come here, these barbarians, to teach us architecture—we, who are the sons of Michelangelo." ITALIAN EDUCATOR.

"The Russians used to rape eighty-year-old women . . . And after that, instead of being sick they simply drank vodka. You [Americans] wouldn't do that, I'm sure. You give them chocolates and contraceptives when you make love to them . . . Every people has its own customs. But don't worry. You'll never feel sick, whatever you do . . ." From VIRGIL GHEORGHIU's *The Twenty-fifth Hour*—Europe's No. 1 fiction best-seller.

". . . American influence has been harmful, for it has already begun the scaling down of aesthetic values so as to be within the intellectual grasp of the average city dweller . . . [it] will end, not with the debasement of taste, but with the disappearance of the word from our vocabulary." MARTIN COOPER; B.B.C. broadcast.

"Thus, if France allows itself to be influenced by the whole of American culture, a living and liveable situation there will come here and completely shatter our cultural traditions . . ." JEAN-PAUL SARTRE; *A European Declaration of Independence.*

"Jazz is their music, comic strips their most admired pictures, magazine stories their literature, Hollywood films their most popular entertainment, skyscrapers their architecture and their newest ball-point pen can write under water . . . We know, too, that God could make America a wonderful country if he only had the money." GEORGE MIKES in *How to Scrape Skies.*

"America—the only country that's gone from barbarism to decadence without being civilized in the meantime." ANONYMOUS.

Well, there they are—all the horrors, mythological or real, synchronizing in the one theme of spiritual impoverishment. Only recently have we begun doing something about it. After leaving the field to the Russians at first, we authorized the State Department in 1948 to set up an "information and educational exchange program," and within a year this was further supplemented when ECA's information program was organized. We remained pikers, however. And it wasn't until after Korea that Congress decided that a "Campaign of Truth" was in order and voted the money to get it going.

Will we get our money's worth? In view of the recent rise in American unpopularity it is easy to assume that our propaganda dollars are going down the drain. But the feeling of futility is unwarranted—certainly if ECA had been a complete propaganda failure there would be no "neutralism" problem in Europe to worry about.

We're fairly new to the game, but—as even the avuncular British concede—we have been learning fast. We are ready to turn pro.

What have we learned? First, that we need much more of a sharpshooting approach to our "target" groups. There is no "European mind," but scores of group attitudes compounded along all sorts of professional, economic, and geographic lines. And the best way to get at them is through people that talk the separate lingoes. We have had a hard time talking to European intellectuals, for example, yet so far we have used few intellectuals for the job. The work of our "labor diplomats," in the toughest sector of the fight, underlines the same moral. How do they go about it? "You talk to the brothers," says one of them. "You go around and you talk to the brothers."

Next, we have learned that one of the principal reasons for the disbelief in American culture is, simply, the high cost of it. Stroll along the Kaertnerstrasse in Vienna, for example, and you will have a hard time finding a bookstore with any decent assortment of moderately priced American books *in German*—that is, until you come to the Communist information center, which has quite an interesting selection. Because of the lack of financial guarantees, European publishers have been loath to publish translations of anything except our sure-fire sex-and-mayhem fiction. So with the theatre; stiff royalties—payable in dollars—have inhibited widespread production of U.S. plays, and while the American companies that have gone over have dispelled a lot of European delusions, they have been far too few to make a profound impression. Patently, if we wish to project American culture rather than talk about it, a much more vigorous subsidy program is in order.

More important, we must develop far better means of reaching the masses. Considerable ingenuity has been brought to this problem; our people have put documentary films into thousands of commercial theatres, taken them in trailers to rural villages, brought "showboats" to Mediterranean coastal towns, subsidized troubadours to sing our story in Sicily, floated message-bearing toy balloons all over Europe, distributed household pamphlets and comic books by the millions. But though it is difficult to think of a bet that has been overlooked, we have made only a dent.

Why don't we merely expand all this? The answer, unfortunately, is not that simple. Europe has had a bellyful of propaganda these last ten years, and after a certain point—and it is a very arguable point—you run not only into diminishing returns but rapidly increasing resistance.

There is, however, a way out of the dilemma—the participation of foreign nations in the job. "Let me get the facts about Korea to one pro-U.S. union man over here," says a U.S. propagandist, "and he'll be worth a thousand posters." There are many ways to invoke this aid. But there is one so effective, so destructive of the myth, that it has come to be the most promising weapon in our whole armory.

It was in Paris in the summer of 1948; Sir Stafford Cripps and ECA boss Paul Hoffman were talking about productivity. How, Cripps asked, did the Americans do it? It

223

was a question to delight a salesman's heart. "Let's bring your people over," Hoffman answered, "and we'll show them how."

So, with great vigor, we proceeded to do. Before long U.S. firms, labor unions, and professional groups were playing host to scores of European "productivity teams"; by the end of last year over 2,750 had made the trip and returned home—somewhat numbed, but enthusiastic—to tell what they had learned. The result, in increased productivity, is now a well-known story—and a good story it is. But there is another story that is not so well known.

What was conceived of as a technical measure turned out to be one of the most effective propaganda tools ever handed us. What was it the Yanks had over there? Was it, as people had said, the number of gadgets and gimmicks we had? Fortuitous national resources? Ruthlessness and overwork? Or was it something more profound? We gave Europeans a chance to come over and *discover for themselves*. And gained ourselves disciples.

Here—in excerpts from productivity-team reports—are some of the things they had to say to their countrymen.

"A visit to the U.S. gives one greater confidence in the ability of democracy to solve its problems . . . The country is still . . . moving *forward* both culturally, socially, and economically."
(*Norwegian trade-unionists*)

"American unions' attitude to company profits is typical of their acceptance of a capitalist economy. However high, profits, at least in competitive industry, are not regarded as immoral or a social evil; indeed they give proof of solvency and assured employment . . . the main concern of unions is to obtain a fair share of them."
(*British trade-union officials*)

"Contrary to the impression gained from many American films, only a small percentage of American workers and their families live in tenements." (*British trade-union officials*)

"There appeared to be a most friendly and genuine attitude of co-operation between management and labor and suggestions made by one side appeared to receive careful consideration, and in most cases support, from the other." (*British rayon-weaving team*)

"The relations between management and labor in the great majority of mills which we visited were excellent. There was often a sense of camaraderie based on mutual respect . . ."
(*British cotton-spinning team*)

"Sometimes we had to ask ourselves whether it was manufacturer or union member speaking to us."
(*Danish ready-made-clothing team*)

"The big surprise to me was the importance American bosses give to human-relations problems. The American employer seems to be a psychologist aware that his prosperity is tied directly with that of the workers." (*French unionist*)

"Both management and labor have taken steps to give greater efficiency in production and more understanding in relationships. When we return to Belgium I intend to recommend better management-labor relationships be created in our mines. I will see that this is done at Charbonnages de Houthalen, the mine I am managing." (*Belgian coal-mining team*)

"If members of the team had learned nothing else from their travels in America and Britain, they would have learned one valuable thing, namely, the remarkable amount of good will which exists between people in the Western Hemisphere."
(*British gray-iron-founding team*)

It is difficult for an American to appreciate what revolutionary documents these are. The British trade-union officials' report, for example, became a front-page story and gave British labor a resounding intellectual jolt. The Norwegian report, coupled with the report of a similar team that went to Russia, opened the eyes of left-wingers in a way that all the money in the world would not buy us. Throughout Europe, on a small but appreciable scale, doctrinaires of one kind or another are being provoked to rethink long and dearly held conceptions.

What gives the reports their impact? In an indirect way, the answer is to be found in the very criticisms they make. The teams make it plain that there are a good many aspects of the American Way of Life that they believe are either undesirable—the pace, for example—or inapplicable. But this leads them to a more important observation. These are only particulars, they say to their countrymen; they are not organic; the essentials of the American success can be had without them. And that is exactly the theme of the present book.

The technical-assistance teams are only one of the ways we have to go about the job of clarification. Thanks to the machinery set up in 1946 and 1948 by the Fulbright and Smith-Mundt acts, and to special programs for Germany, Austria, Finland, China, and Iran, State is bringing over students, teachers, professional people, specialists, and "leaders." The Defense Department is doing the same with Japan. Both State and ECA are placing foreign trainees in U.S. industry, farms, and government agencies. Altogether, the government is now bringing over about 13,000 people a year for observation, study, teaching, training, and indoctrination. Cost: about $45 million.

But by far the biggest contribution of all has been made by private organizations. This year they will have arranged roughly 40,000 exchanges of their own, and in addition will have footed a large share of the local expenses of many of the people brought over by the State Department. The 4-H clubs have been exchanging young farmers; the Rotary clubs have been bringing over students; the Girl Scouts, "youth leaders"—the list encompasses almost every kind of organization in American community life.

Measured against the need, however, our over-all exchange effort has been piddling.* There is a sort of geometric progression inherent to this kind of exchange; since the clue to its success is *applying* the Proposition, it follows that the more people engaged in it, the more effective each individual's work becomes. It has been very frustrating for many middle-management people, for example, to return to Europe all steamed up about, say, labor-management councils, only to realize that no one else in the outfit has got the word. Like plasma, exchange is best in massive doses.

We have a tremendous opportunity before us. We should seize it by expanding our total propaganda budget to at least $500 million a year—and of this devote at least $180 million to exchange. We could not legislate a bigger bargain for ourselves. For every government dollar we put in the exchange kitty, we stimulate at least two matching dollars from private groups here and organizations and governments on the other side. As a result, by priming the pump with $180 million, we could step up the exchange to roughly 50,000 people a year to the U.S.; at least 10,000 in the other direction.

---

* Note: Koreans brought to Moscow between 1946 and 1949: 2,600. Brought to U.S. in same period: 65.

Mere expansion, of course, is not enough. Much more follow-up is needed abroad; equally important, much more preparation on this side. Exposure to America, as we have learned, does not itself produce understanding. The Mayor of Graz is a case in point; when he got back he wrote the State Department that the Communist claim of imminent American bankruptcy might be correct—he had noticed that almost everyone in America seemed to be buying on the installment plan. To do the job properly we should greatly extend our present system of "orientation centers," and develop more provisions for working the stranger into community life. Here again, we have a tremendous asset in our private organizations. Already they are doing a tremendous job in welcoming and shepherding strangers, taking them on historical tours and plant trips, shepherding them to P.T.A. and town meetings, and, in general, making them feel at home. And it is this, it might be added, that visitors talk about most often when they get home.

What has impressed the visitor points a moral for us as well. For when we assess our whole communication effort we find that, as in industry's communication effort, participation lies at the heart of our successes. It is not merely a question of manufacturing "propaganda." Nor is it merely a government matter. The problem encompasses all of us—for it is only as the diverse groups that make up our society *get involved* in the job that our words carry real dynamism. And the potential is tremendous. U.S. business, for example, has already contributed to our communication effort, but there is still more to be done. For the one area that remains virtually untouched is the one area for which U.S. business is the best-qualified group in all the world: getting the American idea across to European *top* management. It is hardly necessary to suggest the means; there could be seminars and international conventions—organizations such as the International C. of C. are ready-made for this—trips and private exchanges of all sorts; and, as the success of the sales troupe "Red" Motley took to England suggests, some good old-fashioned barnstorming as well.

The more fields one thinks of, the more opportunities become evident. Labor, for example, is fairly bursting its seams to do more missionary work in Europe—and the more this is encouraged, the quicker will we reach European labor. So with all of our groups. The success of our communication efforts will depend ultimately on *private* initiative. And this is the way it must be. The American revolution is a challenge, not to states, but to free men, whose never-ending task is to seize their opportunities.

U.S. FOREIGN POLICY

THE ART OF FOREIGN POLICY deals with essentially
tragic materials: war; hard choices between evils,
or between an inimical good and best; the special vanity
and brutishness of human nature when it acts as a national crowd. History's bloodiest pages are its international pages; the ugliest passions of man are the daily
coin of diplomacy. This is no art for amateurs, altruists,
or even optimists. Democracies seem always at a special
disadvantage in it.

Despite their native political talent, Americans have
been awkward and unsuccessful in foreign policy since
about 1917. This is not to say that our talent stops at the
water's edge; nor is there much truth in Will Rogers' saying that the U.S. never lost a war or won a conference.
Before 1917 our foreign policy was mainly successful
and occasionally brilliant. Its problem was simpler. The
world's policeman was the Navy of our cousin, Britain,
with whom our quarrels after 1815 were trivial or sentimental. U.S. statesmen could and did push U.S. ideals

and U.S. national interests alike with no great reason for misgivings about their compatibility. Our single experience of political tragedy was domestic (1861–1865). We were, in the main, too successful to worry much or long; professors did not urge us (as Crane Brinton now does) to become a "pessimistic democracy," nor would most Americans have taken such advice.

But since 1917, failures and misgivings have been our steady diet, washed down with two epochal crusades. This can be explained, if not justified, by a vast change in the structure and nature of the political world. No sooner had America "matured" as a world power than two other great events changed the rules by which we had grown up. The world of many balanced "great powers" began re-forming into a world of two or three super powers, the rest shriveling; and it also entered what historians call another revolutionary age. The latter change, heralded by Lenin and advanced by Hitler and Stalin, has been described by Charles Sabine as "the advent of political theories which reject the obligation to be reasonable." So the U.S. entered big-league politics just when the premises of its civilization were repudiated and challenged by ideas that attached themselves to some of the most militarily formidable nations in history.

To compound these troubles of fate, the American people or their statesmen have committed at least three major blunders in the last thirty years, blunders by the diplomatic standards of any age, "revolutionary" or not:

1. Wrongly pretending that Britain (or somebody) was still policing the post-Versailles world, we sought

an unarmed, uneconomic, and irresponsible isolation (1920–1940) of a kind quite foreign to our traditions.

2. In the midst of a war of principle as well as of survival we adopted an unprincipled and dangerous war aim, unconditional surrender (1943); and compounded it with unprincipled and dangerous concessions at Tehran and Yalta.

3. Before the task of peacemaking was complete or even well begun, we demobilized (1945–1950).

Many sub-blunders could be added, notably our strange and disastrous China policy since 1946. A few successes, while strictly defensive, have pierced the gloom, such as ECA and the Berlin airlift. But our blunders were huge and classic affronts to elementary rules of power politics that earlier generations of American statesmen, beginning with Washington, Hamilton, and Jefferson, knew by instinct. These rules were succinctly put the other day by McGeorge Bundy: "Policy cannot be unprincipled and it cannot go unarmed." To which he added, "But it must come first."

Can such rules light us through the dangerous mess we are in now? The present Secretary of State describes his job as "shepherding dilemmas." Most of these dilemmas are procedural. Never was America so nearly unanimous on the fact that it has a mortal enemy; never was it in such a quandary about how to proceed. The current debate (Hoover, Dulles, Taft, etc.) has raised interesting problems of means—our arms and our diplomacy—but has not enlightened the question of our national goals, which arms and diplomacy alike should serve. If the goal were merely to *survive* World War III, preserving what Mr. Hoover calls "a stronghold of Christian civilization in the world," his proposals might warrant consideration. Survival, of course, is a pre-condition to the fulfillment of any goal. But from what has been presented in this book concerning the meaning and development of the U.S., it must be clear that survival itself does not begin to define an adequate one. So before we turn to operational problems, let us consider U.S. foreign policy in somewhat broader terms. This requires taking our eye off Stalin for a moment, and reviewing our traditional purposes in foreign affairs and the contemporary bearings of the American Proposition.

In the days of the Pax Britannica, U.S. statesmen helped the country not only to survive but to grow in territory and strength by some very neat footwork among the powerful chancelleries of Europe. They also, under the British umbrella, announced and defended the Monroe Doctrine, and later promulgated John Hay's Open Door. The Open Door doctrine, though it started with China, was meant to be as universal as the Monroe Doctrine was regional; Teddy Roosevelt tried to apply it to North Africa (1906) and it was the direct ancestor of Wilson's wholly global policy of "self-determination for all peoples" at Versailles.

In advancing these doctrines U.S. statesmen were advancing U.S. interests and U.S. principles at the same time. They could justly claim that our particular objective—whether to keep the Romanovs out of the West Coast, or the Bourbons out of Latin America, or a Bonaparte out of Mexico—would be accompanied by and justified by an advance of human freedom. With intervals of backsliding and distortion, this higher purpose, or test, of our policies is the most consistent single thread in U.S. history. Every Secretary of State has at least paid it lip service; according to Dean Acheson, "The most affirmative truth we hold is the dignity and right of every nation, every people, every individual to develop in their own way." Controversy has centered around the question, not whether the U.S. has this mission of freedom, but whether in a perilous world it should confine its espousal to the setting of a good example. From the time of the Mexican War, which Congressman Lincoln opposed, and more particularly from the time of our war with Spain, many an intelligent apostle of liberty (such as William James, Charles Beard, and recently Clinton Rossiter) has deplored U.S. "foreign meddling" even in freedom's name, on the ground that freedom is better served by being cultivated at home. The current version of this controversy is how much rearmament America can stand without becoming a "garrison state."

But whenever U.S. statesmen have sought to influence world affairs by something more than exhortation and example—i.e., by power—they have had to take some risks with liberty. They have had to take exactly the same risks that our Founding Fathers took when, knowing that all governments are natural enemies of liberty, they decided to set one up nevertheless. And like the founders, our later statesmen confronted the first political law of liberty: it can survive only when power is controlled. The search for ways to control power, and a generalized hostility to all uncontrolled power, therefore constitute the second consistent thread in U.S. foreign policy. So far we know only two ways to control power: by law, or by diffusion (checks and balances). As we use both ways to protect liberty in our own government, so we have tried both in our foreign affairs.

Law is the preferred way, because when law is thought just, and so commands consent, it can be enforced with a very small police force. In this conviction the U.S. has always shown a solemn regard for international law, and has done almost as much as the Dutch, the Colombians, and other small nations to foment the impression that international law is a real and growing force in world affairs. This line of policy has been genuinely successful in the hospitable climate of Latin America, where international affairs are now less governed by the fear of force than by the hope of justice under the judicial and arbitral procedures of the Inter-American Conference and its Pan American Union. Woodrow Wilson also went to Europe with the banner of law; his League of Nations was to *make* international law by consulting "world opinion," and then enforce it by collective security. This was the noblest, if not the shrewdest, idea Americans had yet offered on the big stage. The same quest produced the Kellogg Pact, and was in the minds of the authors of the Hoover-Stimson non-recognition doctrine. In 1945 the desirability of a strong international law was so taken for granted by the American people that only two Senators, Langer and Shipstead, voted against ratification of the U.N. The veto provision made it possible for the Senate to avoid debating whether the *sine qua non* of any successful legal system—a common vocabulary of right and wrong—existed in the world of 1945 or not.

It is worth pausing a moment over this American passion for law. We have trusted to it even when we knew it was unenforceable. During nearly a hundred years of our history (1829 to 1924) the daily routine of U.S. foreign policy was virtually controlled by two unknown foreign-service officers, William Hunter and A. A. Adee. As second assistant secretaries or less, these men drafted or passed on all our diplomatic notes and communications. Their chief, if not their only, equipment for this important task was (according to historian T. A. Bailey) their "remarkable knowledge of precedent, international law, and diplomatic procedure." That legalistic tradition hangs over the State Department today. It is not altogether silly. Its practical assumption is that law can be strengthened by repeated observance, and develops a moral inhibitory effect on national policies as the precedents pile up. Its idealistic assumption is that there is a natural harmony among the real interests of different nations which law most nearly expresses. In international affairs, as in domestic, Americans retain an instinctive belief in a law behind the law—"natural law," as it used to be called— which is easier to enforce when found, because it is to everybody's long-term interest. Despite the acids poured on this notion by Justice Holmes and his followers, it keeps coming back, a recent example being Adolf Berle's arresting hypothesis of "natural selection of political forces," a kind of moral Darwinism of politics. The idea of natural law—being no more mystical than the belief in the possibility of justice—will not die as long as Americans are true to their optimistic traditions, and they will keep trying to export it, too. It inspired the foolish faith in the U.N. of 1945; it also inspired the American decision to reverse a prior decision of our own military strategists and defend Korea in June, 1950.

This "Wilsonian" complex of ideas—a natural harmony supported by reason and public opinion—was so powerful that it bemused the world's democratic statesmen for twenty years after the revolutionary age had begun. It took Hitler's worst to revive the pessimistic resolution necessary to defeat him, and it took several years after San Francisco for most Westerners to realize that Stalin also does not fit under such rules. Americans should have known better, for their traditional foreign policy, like their domestic system, has had its pessimistic side too.

Unchecked and growing power, however distant, has always put Americans in a belligerent mood. Instead of waiting for them to be actively frightened, as by a fall of France, or of China, a few farsighted U.S. statesmen have played the preventive diplomacy called the balance of power. It is, of course, the method by which British foreign policy maximized its influence for four hundred years. Teddy Roosevelt, among twentieth-century Americans, adopted it vigorously. His Treaty of Portsmouth (1905) was deliberately arranged to prevent conclusive victory from destroying the balance between Japan and Russia in Asia. Although Wilson piously denounced the balance of power as obsolete and evil, his 1920 Siberian venture had the balancing purpose of checking Japan there. Stimson's non-recognition of Manchukuo could have claimed similar insight, had it been backed by force at the time. Since World War II the change in the pattern of power has obscured this basic principle. Even Britain has stopped trying to "balance Europe" (*i.e.*, as between France and Germany). It takes a continent to balance a continent nowadays, and Europe cannot balance anything unless Europe is united first. But our national instinct for the balance of power survives. It led Senator Lodge to write the purpose of European unification into the ECA Act. It even keeps the State Department peering toward Peiping for signs of "Titoism" in the Mao regime.

Europe is not united, and Mao is no Tito. These, our two biggest problems of balance, are both failures. Our other policy, the promotion of world law, is also being discredited by the poltroonery and inherent weaknesses of the U.N. In this crisis either or both policies are in danger of being abandoned. Mr. Hoover's islanded Maginot, which has room for neither, wins a large following; on the other hand, the proponents of various kinds of world government, brandishing the A bomb and their premature constitution, shout, "We told you so," and gather new recruits.

Yet if the world is ever to have peace with freedom, these traditional American methods of controlling power are still the only way to secure it. A world government will be a tolerable government only if it is supported by a common sense of justice (a world government now, as E. B. White says, would resemble a "consolidation of Alcatraz and Brearley") and by a well-dispersed pattern of national powers. To promote these American aims is to advance toward the possibility of a tolerable world government. That, under various names, from "the liberation of mankind" to Whitman's "vistas of coming humanity," has been and should remain our long-term national objective.

So much for our classical goals. It was necessary to restate them in order to be clear that they are not responsible for the danger we are now in. It is often said that the trouble with our foreign policy is a question of goals, but evidently, insofar as the classical ones are concerned, this is not the case. The question still remains open, of course, as to whether these goals are adequate for our time; whether we may not need to formulate something more capacious, something more serviceable to the kind of domestic aims that have been set forth, for example, in this book. This question requires an answer. But it is rash to seek that answer without first realizing that the failure of U.S. foreign policy, as it stands today, is *primarily* a failure at the operating level; a failure of the men, policies, and institutions that should be serving our goals (whether classical or new) and are not. This important fact is borne out by closer observation.

Of all the dilemmas Mr. Acheson shepherds, only one is not just procedural. That is the question of coexistence: should we entertain the possibility that the U.S. and Soviet Russia can ever get along in the same world? There is little doubt that State Department policy (which has been described as "enforced coexistence and defensive containment") implies the hope that the Kremlin will someday forswear or moderate its Leninist vows. This assumption keeps us vulnerable to the familiar Communist hot-cold tactic. Stalin says hopes-up, and our hopes of peace do go up—only to plunge later on. But as Mr. Acheson himself has said, quoting Dr. Charles Malik of Lebanon, "There can be no greater disagreement than when someone wants to eliminate your existence altogether." The only hope of survival against such a foe is to take an equal and opposite resolve against his existence.

This logic requires a more precise definition of the foe. The foe is not the Russian nation (still less the Russian people), for coexistence with a Russian nation, even a Russian nation organized along Soviet lines, is perfectly possible under a rational government that is not committed to the Communization of the world by any and all means. Is international Communism the enemy, then? Yes, but not in itself a very terrifying one; it is a mortal enemy only when it controls an apparatus the size of the Russian or Chinese nation. International Communism, as an idea with no wringable neck, can be defeated by superior ideas when its only vehicle is the minds of free men. It is the combination of irrational dogma and national power that is the really mortal enemy. This combination has its peak in the Kremlin gang. Stalin, the Politburo, and a few hundred other men, armed as they are with the might of Russia and Eastern Europe, and their junior partners in Asia, are the mortal enemies of the free world. As they are determined to destroy it, so it must determine to be rid of them. The rest is procedure.

If this reasoning is accepted, the U.S. has both a long-term and a short-term national objective: (1) a world in which individual and national freedom is protected by law and a healthy diffusion of power; (2) the removal of the chief visible obstacle to such a world, the power of the Kremlin gang. The procedural dilemmas are best solved by men, institutions, and policies that serve both these aims at once.

To begin with the institutions. John Hay used to maintain petulantly that the Constitution plus the two-party system made his treaty-making job impossible, since "there will always be 34 per cent of the Senate on the blackguard side of every question." (Hay's best treaties were ratified, however; some dubious ones weren't.) Despite the wider use of executive agreements, and the great exfoliation of new functions and agencies of foreign policy (from ECA to the Voice of America) with wide operating leeway, Hay's problem is still with us, greatly enlarged in scale and tempo. Democracy *is* a handicap to diplomacy, especially against a totalitarian adversary. Public and congressional opinion, even when they coincide with each other, are often slower to change than the right moves in the chess game require—moves that may need great flexibility and secrecy to boot. Advocates of the parliamentary system see no cure for this short of giving the State Department the same degree of leeway the British Foreign Office has, at the same time making it wholly responsible to Congress instead of to the President.

Since Stettinius' time, State has made great efforts to improve its public and congressional relations. Its Public Liaison Division gives regular briefing sessions to some

200 organizations affecting public opinion, and Mr. Acheson, an effective speaker, does not stint his energies in telling the voters what he is trying to do. The applause he has received from the public does not offset the glares he still gets from the Senate. This may mean a flaw in our system. But if there is anything seriously wrong with him or his policies the case is not proved—rather the opposite: the system is working. And even if his policies are right, the case against our system should not be over-stated. Its flaw, if any, is that it does not work well in the absence of strong leadership.

As to the men: most or all of the 24,000 employees of our State Department, from the Secretary down, are hard-working and conscientious public servants, neither pansies nor traitors. Some of them are very able; Mr. Acheson himself was as well equipped for the difficult technical aspects of the job of Under Secretary as any public servant in years. Yet the case against those re-sponsible for recent U.S. foreign policy is prima facie overwhelming: their policies, whether right or wrong in themselves, have obviously not been good enough. If our enormous resources of power and prestige had been cor-rectly deployed since 1945, we could not possibly be in such a mess now. Somebody has been steadily misunder-standing either the true nature of the world or the true interests of the U.S., or both. This, rather than "isolation-ism" or partisan bias, explains the chronic suspicion on the Hill toward the State Department in general; and since Mr. Acheson has been there for most of the past five years, his regime necessarily inherits the mistrust along with the mistakes.

At the risk of oversimplifying the thought processes of a large group of men, we may note three blind spots that seem characteristic of the dominant State Department crowd today. The first, which goes back to Franklin Roosevelt, is a failure to realize that the old nineteenth-century categories of "left" and "right" are no longer meaningful in a revolutionary age, and have become mere hooks by which the propagandists of political unreason, disguised as "leftists" and "rightists," try to pull free nations apart. The stereotype of Stalin (and now of Mao) as a "leftist," a spokesman of reforms and therefore of the future, undoubtedly delayed the department's recognition of him as an enemy. And it was not the trained men of the department but a couple of politicians, Senator Vandenberg and Secretary Byrnes, who first saw the light and called the turn. Per contra, an old-fashioned right-wing warlord like Chiang Kai-shek was mistakenly branded a "Fascist," although the political thought behind his (Sun Yat-sen's) revolution has no tincture of Fascist unreason. It was the State Department that sought to introduce unreason into Chiang's regime by sponsoring an impossible coalition with the Communists. If this intellectual blind spot does not explain what even State now terms "the China mistake," then one must suspect an equally blind personal hatred toward Chiang.

A second blind spot in the department is an aloofness or indifference to U.S. private business, union labor, and the economic system that both represent. Although every embassy now has labor attachés, they are not used or regarded as our front-line diplomatic troops among the world's working classes, which are international Communism's first objective. The A.F. of L., by giving money and backing to its anti-Communist brethren abroad, has done far more effective work than the State Department on this front. Businessmen also look to State in vain for support, leadership, or even ordinary savvy in foreign economic affairs. The system of private capitalism, and the rules under which it can flourish, have not been promoted or even very strongly defended during the era of "donation diplomacy." Necessary as the latter was, it need not have been a substitute for a simultaneous attack on the underlying problem of workable economic relations with the world. Nor does the Gray report, made belatedly outside the department, fill this gap.

A third blind spot is a reluctance to grasp or use all the levers of power through which policy becomes operationally effective. There are still U.S. diplomats who refuse, for example, to have anything to do with propaganda. At this moment there is a glaring opportunity for *operational* diplomacy that would result in the killing of Communists, the discomfiture of Mao, and indirect aid to our Korean forces and to de Lattre's in Indo-China: namely, assistance to Chinese anti-Communist guerrillas on the mainland. No legal or moral barriers preclude such aid; it could be sent with or without the use of Formosan channels. But State has not even given the guerrillas Voice of America support!

Such inaction has many excuses; the feeblest is "non-intervention." This obsolete doctrine, which was developed by Castlereagh to get out of playing Metternich's game, assumes a discontinuity between domestic and foreign rights that may have existed in a monarchic age but does not now. As used in the department, it is almost always a shibboleth betraying the diplomat who believes that Britain (or somebody) is still keeping world peace. Anything it ever meant is now better expressed by "self-determination." As Justice Douglas has put it, "American influence makes and breaks governments. . . . We have been interfering for years and must continue to do so if the tide of Communism is to be turned."

Mr. Acheson and his cohorts are, of course, thorough-going Anglophiles. This in itself is not a heinous blind spot at a time when our British alliance is a cornerstone of policy. As a habit of mind, however, Anglophilia has one danger. It fosters the illusion that close association with Englishmen—pleasant and desirable as that is on other grounds—conveys by a kind of osmosis the great wisdom of the British in foreign affairs. That wisdom is worth emulating, and many aspects of the old Pax Britannica foreign policy also have application to U.S. problems today. But the British now have a paler policy, and their views on many of our common problems, from the convertibility of the pound to the importance of Asia, can be no substitute for the original thinking and action that must lead to an American peace.

There are cases—as in Mr. Attlee's recent visit—where we have taken a strong stand apart from Great Britain. There are cases where we should but have not. A good example of where original American thought and action are needed right now is "the forgotten theatre," the Middle East. This strategic area is not only Russia's own soft underbelly, but the source of Europe's oil; a

Soviet assault on it would be as serious to Europe as an assault on the Ruhr. Moreover, a policy of constructive balance of power would see this vast and populous region as a potential unity from which the voice of the Arab people will someday speak strongly in the councils of the great. Arab unity should be an objective of U.S. policy—not only for another of the "situations of strength" Mr. Acheson desires, but for the sake of a better-balanced world. U.S. Near Eastern policy, however, has no such coherent goal. It is the frazzled sum of half measures. Our Palestine policy, made in the White House for a handful of Zionists, has left us with an untended legacy of Arab disillusion and Arab refugees. We have successfully built up Turkey, but without coordinating its defense with that of its Near Eastern neighbors, especially Iran. In Iran, indeed, we have not yet decided whether a Red Army invasion could be resisted or not, and have sent only enough military aid to make the country feel comparatively neglected. State Department men responsible for this area also feel neglected by the spotlight of history, complaining that it will be impossible to arouse preventive interest in their problems until Russia arouses it— when it will be too late. Meanwhile there is a disposition to leave the Middle East to the British, who, however, have no plan either for its future or for its over-all defense.

Such are some of the operational fronts on which U.S. foreign policy must become more effective and more forehanded. But is the policy itself wrong in any respect?

The basic policy of the Truman Administration is the

Truman Doctrine, announced when Great Britain had to abandon the Greek civil war in 1947. It states that the U.S. will "support free people who are resisting attempted subjugation by armed minorities or by outside pressures" so that they can remain free "to work out their own destinies in their own way." The Truman Doctrine in effect promises military and economic aid to any and all victims of Communist aggression. It is a noble doctrine in direct line of descent and development from the doctrines of Monroe and Hay and Wilson's "self-determination." It has since been seriously qualified, if not gutted, by the Acheson corollary: that U.S. aid will be supplied only when it is the "missing component" in a situation that has all the other ingredients of success (will to resist, defensibility, etc.). But its more obvious limitation is the inability of the U.S. to supply adequate aid in all the places where Communist aggression can start. It is therefore not a fully successful policy. Teddy Roosevelt, the last *successful* operator in the field, said, "I never take a step in foreign policy unless I am assured that I shall be able eventually to carry out my will by force."

There are two ways to bring the Truman Doctrine into closer accord with reality and make it successful. The first, which we are pursuing, is to rearm ourselves and our allies (especially NATO) as fast as possible, with the ultimate purpose of being able to stop Communism anywhere at all. The only question about this method is whether we are pursuing it fast enough. The second way is to wrap the Truman Doctrine in the flag of the U.N., applying it only in cases where we have the U.N.'s clear mandate, as in Korea. This, an interim method, would enable the U.S. to tailor its commitments to its military capacity, for if the U.N. asked more than we could deliver, we could in turn demand more of the other members of the U.N. Meanwhile we could use our weight in the U.N. on behalf of 100 per cent courage and correctness (as in respect to Chinese aggression) in order to keep a clean legal record even if the force is temporarily lacking. Such a policy, which sounds legalistic and hypocritical, would not be so if we are resolved to vindicate it in the long run. It would be in the best American tradition of bolstering law—*provided* it is not used as a cover for our own irresolution or fear of involvement. Correct positions, even "unrealistic" ones (Stimson's non-recognition of Manchukuo, the U.N.'s reluctant but continued recognition of Chiang, our own of Lithuania, etc.), sometimes grow enforceable with time.

The U.S. can make them enforceable, however, only by directing the whole of its policy to that end. For example, the balance of power (if nothing else) requires that someone other than Stalin control the foreign policy of China. Until Mr. Acheson sees this as a political necessity instead of something to hope for, our Asian policy will continue to be a failure. If our policy is really not to overthrow Mao but to hope that he will someday fall out with Stalin—then our U.N. maneuvers to declare Mao the aggressor are Pecksniffian indeed.

Our need for allies against Stalin is of course absolute, and our policy is rightly directed toward rallying them. Yet they are not best rallied by a policy that, like the Acheson corollary, picks and chooses among non-Communist governments, or, like recent Senate speeches, assesses their moral fiber. All free nations are our natural allies; each of them is an American front; and leadership consists partly of assuming that they harbor enough courage to follow. There is no country in the world today, including Russia, where significant enemies of Stalin do not exist and await leadership.

This leadership also has the task of making clear why, and in what sense, we believe in a balance of power. The very phrase has a chilly sound to many Americans, though it is in itself neither moral nor immoral. If we use it merely as a tool to maintain American power, then it may slip in our hands. Its moral use is to hold open the door of history for a while—perhaps in what Crane Brinton calls "the last hegemony"—until we can be sure that the coming world government will be the kind in which liberty is safe. A surer vision of that developing world is essential to the conduct of successful foreign policy. It would have saved us from the error and consequences of "unconditional surrender" in Germany and Japan. It will warn us away from Mr. Churchill's desperate plan of forcing Stalin, under the threat of atomic war, to "make a deal" (which would have to be at some innocent nation's expense). It will also stay our hand from releasing bombs on the Kremlin, if ever, until we have some clearer ideas on how this maneuver would be followed up, and what we would like to see in Stalin's place.

But the balance of power, however necessary, cannot be the whole of our policy. A reign of law requires, not only healthy pluralism, but also something like a "world community," toward the growth of which each nation contributes what it best can. And the American character and tradition will never be satisfied with a merely defensive or even preventive foreign policy. We seek ways to be creative and constructive—ways in which we can feel we are extending the American Proposition to other peoples. Such ways exist.

Our most conspicuous current asset, which the rest of the world badly needs, is economic: not just wealth but the secret of creating it. The ECA, our best-conducted foreign economic operation, is living proof that to share wealth is not necessarily to share its secret. Before it was swamped by Europe's rearmament, it had succeeded in saving Europe's economy and pointing it toward a precarious "viability"; but it had not succeeded in reforming European capitalism or giving it a new horizon of economic progress. Thus the standard of living of French industrial workers, in spite of all the ECA-inspired new industrial investment, remained as low or lower than before the war, and they have little more stake in France's economic present or future than they had in 1788.

If U.S. capitalism is ever to perform its task of raising living standards in the so-called "backward" areas of the world, it will need the cooperation of European industry just as surely as our military strategy requires Europe's steel. The British Commonwealth's Colombo plan, for example, could be a convenient device for the subcontracting of part of our own enormous Point Four opportunities in Southeast Asia. But unless we are merely to pick up the check for another experiment in state planning, this arrangement must be preceded by some degree of assimilation among the three great centers of Western industrial strength, Britain's, continental Europe's, and ours. It is now clear that there will never be an economic or military integration of Britain and Europe (or even of Europe alone) except as they march together toward economic integration with the U.S. in an Atlantic Community. The most skillful "donation diplomacy," Payments Union, Schuman plan, and all could not break up the nest of little obsolete autarchies that Europe insists on retaining until it has something better in sight.

These considerations lead us back from the question of operations to that of goals. The classical goals mentioned earlier in this chapter can provide a structural base for our new efforts in foreign policy. But it seems clear that, in themselves, they fall short of the contemporary task. If we are to frame our policies aright and speed up the correction of our operational deficiencies, we must build into our foreign relations a goal capable of reinforcing and extending, in a positive and concrete way, the fundamental aims that this book has sought to clarify. The statement of such a goal, with operational techniques to back it, could demolish those troublesome European autarchies, undermine all their dead-end dreams of socialism, and set their extraordinary citizens on a new and more promising path.

The elaboration of such a goal would be a task beyond the proper limits of this book. But surely the essence of it is not far to seek. Old Cordell Hull had an inkling of it. Like other obsolete U.S. policies, the Hull reciprocal-trade treaties were based on Pax Britannica assumptions —in this case the assumption that a world market, which the British had created by their willingness to make a price for any quantity of anything offered for sale, could survive the British withdrawal from that market in the early thirties. A world market will not exist again until another strong nation makes one. We have, as a nation, no adequate incentive to make a true world market. *But we have very good national reasons to extend our own internal free-trade area to certain nations that may be willing to reciprocate.*

An offer of free trade and free migration, coming from the protectionist U.S., would create a sensation in Canada, Britain, Western Europe, or wherever we might feel militarily safe in making it. Since the terms of the offer would require the abandonment of all exchange controls, quantitative restrictions, and other devices that obstruct a progressive division of labor, it would bowl over Europe's socialist politicians like ninepins. The fusing of these markets would intermix men and corporations now walled apart, in such a way that the most successful business practices (by and large the American) would become the prevailing practices throughout the area. Whatever its boundaries, this new super market would be by definition larger and by economic axiom richer than the present U.S.A.

The dislocations for the present U.S. would be considerable. Even some militarily vital industries like chemicals and aluminum would be put at risk. For that reason the free-trade offer, without qualifications, could be made only to nations with which we share a strategic frontier and with whom we feel militarily secure. Such a policy, a major break with the obsolete universality of the Hull approach, would be a new beginning, and would require a radical change in U.S. economic policy. But it is a change that should be made anyway for the sake of American domestic stability, the American taxpayer, and the American manpower supply—which last is already putting too low a ceiling on our own economic and military horizons. It would involve, of course, a passionate congressional debate; for protection is one of our oldest political habits. Yet we have one older one: the habit of extending the American Proposition of freedom as far as our safety permits, and sometimes further. If America is really a system, rather than just another nation, this debate would give us a crucial chance to prove it.

So we should add to our classical goals this new one, of extending the area of our economic freedom, intermixing our people, our blood, and our methods with those of other nations. This, indeed, is what we always used to do, though it is hard to remember, looking backward from the Age of Unreason. Along this line, at any rate, there lies the possibility of evolving a Great Policy and of assuring great political victories in foreign affairs; and some such major effort may well be required of us by the very nature of history's present challenge. For we face not just a gang of villains but a system of evil ideas, and these can be defeated only if we keep our own system of ideas more powerful and more relevant to the real problems of mankind.

Even great policies will not save us from one dismal necessity. The lives we are now losing in Korea are not the last lives we shall lose. It may be we shall have the horrible catharsis of a general war with Russia. It seems as likely, however, that we shall be required to fight a series of partial wars, far short of Armageddon, over remote terrains and over a long period, to maintain the principles of freedom, law, and balance. That may be the hardest test of all: to fight without national hatred or national fear. It may cost us our innocence; foreign policy is a tragic art. It need not cost us our faith.

INDEX

INDEX

257